Theology for the Weak

Yongjea John Han

Copyright © 2018 Yongjea John Han
First edition
Designed and Edited by Canada Christian Society
Vancouver, Canada
All rights reserved. No part of this book may be reproduced or transmitted in any form or by any means, electronic or mechanical, including photocopying and recording, or in any information storage or retrieval system without the prior written permission of CCS Theology Publishing Series.

ISBN-13: 978-1-7750387-8-8

DEDICATION

This book is written for the weak and their mission of North America. Jesus always stood on the side of the weak people of the earth and preached the justice of God and His kingdom.

FOR THE FIRST NATION AND THE WEAK OF THIS LAND

CONTENTS

ACKNOWLEDGMENT 8
PREFACE 9

PART 1

CHAPTER 1   35
CHOSING FAITH AND UNBELIEF
CHAPTER 2   42
WHY SHOULD WE DECIDE TO BELIEVE IN GOD?
CHAPTER 3   49
TRUTH MAKES US FREE
CHAPTER 4   56
OUR FATHER, GOD
CHAPTER 5   62
OUR FATHER, GOD
CHAPTER 6   68
GOD'S PLAN AND REIGN
CHAPTER 7   75
WHO IS JESUS?
CHAPTER 8   80
WHAT JESUS TAUGHT AND DID
CHAPTER 9   86
WHO IS THE HOLY SPIRIT GOD?
CHAPTER 10   91
THE POWER OF THE HOLY SPIRIT

PART 2

CHAPTER 11   98
TRINITY
CHAPTER 12   103
DEPRAVITY AND SALVATION
CHAPTER 13   109
CHANGE
CHAPTER 14   115
THE ENEMY WE SHOULD FIGHT AGAINST
CHAPTER 15   120
THE SECRET OF VICTORY
CHAPTER 16   126
TAKE OFF THE SPIRITUAL SNARE!
CHAPTER 17   132
METHODS OF SPIRITUAL TRAINING
CHAPTER 18   139
DEFINITION OF THE CHURCH
CHAPTER 19   145
SACRAMENTS AND CHURCH WORKERS
CHAPTER 20   153
PRAYER IS A MISSION!

PART 3

CHAPTER 21   159
THE LORD'S PRAYER
CHAPTER 22   164
HOW DO WE KNOW GOD'S WILL?
CHAPTER 23   170
THE MISSION OF THE GOSPEL

CHAPTER 24   177
FAITH, SPIRITUAL HEALTH
CHAPTER 25   183
THE GUARANTEED FUTURE OF THE SAINTS
CHAPTER 26   189
WHERE TO GO IF YOU LEAVE
CHAPTER 27   196
GOING TO THE LORD'S MERIT
CHAPTER 28   202
THE ATTITUDE OF THE OFFERING
CHAPTER 29   208
TO THE END OF THE EARTH,
CHAPTER 30   214
HOW CAN YOU BELIEVE IN SUFFERING?
CHAPTER 31   220
FAITH, WORD AND GRACE

Acknowledgment

I am very pleased to have such a lecture to students who are seeking the truth for the mission of North America. I hope that through this opportunity we will be able to approach theological questions of God, Christ, and the Holy Spirit as well as various theological questions. I would also like to take this lecture to students who would like to walk through learning with me, in a lecture that is beneficial and that will help students to grow their faith. It is a foolish idea to teach students with a short knowledge, but rather it is meaningful to discuss and talk with each other on the theological theme of each other through wide dialogue with students through these opportunities. Rather than reaching a huge theme of theology, we would rather talk about the many challenges we face in our faith life.

PREFACE

IS THEOLOGY A STUDY OF GOD?

God sent His only begotten Son, Jesus Christ, for the weak men of this land. It is important to realize that true theology is a holy journey to learn about God who has looked back at the weak characters. What is theology? But what is the theology as such a topic that we will face and think about in our faith life? These problems are still present in today's world. Theology is also called 'the study about God.' The question then is whether the concept of divine acceptance on earth and in so-called non-Christian countries should be included in this category.

It would be right to define the quest for of God after the definition of what is the concept of God discussed between Christian and non-Christian countries? Theology is the study of God. However, the notion we speak here refers to the concept of God in the Christian position. The definition of God does not fall into the category of theology. Rather, God in theology means God in the Bible and can be regarded as a study of God. In the non-Christian sense, the study about God should be approached from a religious perspective rather than the meaning of theology. Studying religion is a study of God, which is an important medium for the religion, and means theology in all categories that can be interpreted through religion.

The meaning of monotheism in Christianity is defined as God, being only one God. Therefore, it is said through the definition of

God, the only God, that the interpretation of God is the beginning of theology.

God is said to be the God who transcends the Old Testament and the God who is inherent in the New Testament. It is God who has both attributes of transcendence and inheritance. God exists alone, and through Christ he is at the center of the saints, working through the Holy Spirit. How can the only God be working through Christ and the Holy Spirit? It does not violate the idea of the only God at all.

Rather, it becomes a clue to more definitively define it. In other words, God, who is God alone, is expressed in terms of Christ, the Son of God, and God of the Holy Spirit, to teach his attributes more specifically. The God of the Trinity speaks of one attribute and of the other three attributes of the being. God is one, but He completes the ministry of redemption through Christ, the Son, and inherits from transcendence, and again, after the completion of the ministry of Christ, he completes the ministry of redemption as the Holy Spirit. The ministry of the Father, the Son, and the Holy Spirit always goes through the Old Testament and the New Testament completes its ministries.

Therefore, we believe that God, who is the transcendent God in the Old Testament, wants to exist by himself, and God in the New Testament is incarnate through Christ, so that His justice as God who completes the ministries in us is the resurrection of Christ and the ascension of Christ and as a God of the Holy Spirit in the times of the present and the perfection of the completion, we must reinterpret as the God who is both intrinsic and working.

God is transcending. And this God also shows his attributes while accompanying transcendence and intrinsic. This is the completion of this work through the God of the Holy Spirit.

Therefore, without the work of the Holy Spirit and the efforts of the Holy Spirit, the attributes of God do not appear among us. It is the ordinance which God has ordained through Christ, having his attributes among saints.

The Old Testament God is a lawful God, who disciplines his people, hates the sin, and does not tolerate the fornication. The law of God condemns the man and does not guarantee freedom from the law. In the Old Testament, God reveals himself as their God, confined in his own law. But the Old Testament God proclaims the freedom of the law through the New Testament Jesus Christ.

In other words, Jesus Christ was the law itself in the NT. Only those who keep Jesus Christ can receive salvation. It is only through Jesus Christ's revelation that the fulfillment of the law can be accomplished.

Jesus Christ, the Son of God, makes the yoke of the suffering to be taken away and to proclaim freedom by the law. Therefore, God can once again reveal himself through Jesus Christ, the perfection of the law. This is God's self-revelation through Jesus Christ. Second, after God has accomplished the work of Christ's redemption, the God actively intervenes in our life. This is God's 'holy involvement' and 'holy participation.' God actively accomplishes the ministry of the redemption of Christ Jesus, which He has already completed as the Holy Spirit. It is God's intervention into the historical and creative human history.

Therefore, studying theology can be regarded as the search for the justice of God, the God of the Holy Spirit, the ministry of redemption accomplished through this Christ in the human history.

PROOF OF GOD

Can we prove God? We are skeptical about these issues. God is the one who cannot be proved. God is not to be proved, but to know the attributes of God one by one. God is not defined. But God knows who He is. People have made their own efforts to prove God. The representative person would probably be Thomas Aquinas.

He refers to God as a 'proof as a movement,' 'proof as an agent,' and as 'possibility and necessity.' Here, as a movement, the proof is that there is movement in the world, and this movement is exercised by another movement.

This relationship is sustained, and this continuity is endless, and in order to sustain this movement, there is God in the end. Next, to God as a working being, this world must be operated and sustained must have caused. Therefore, it is the story that God exists as this worker and the world is made through that God. Next is the proof of possibility and necessity. This is the story that this world, by itself, does not have a basis for existence, so there may be existent and nonexistent things, that is, there are things that give meaning to such a relationship by the existence of chance and necessity.

Fourth, Thomas says 'step-by-step proof.' It is a step, as it goes up on the stairs, one by one, and proceeds to deduce the existence of God. Fifth, Thomas speaks of 'teleological proof.' This is a proof of

God as the giver of meaning to build order to maintain the order of the world. Sixth is moral proof. It is God who is the one who bestowed it on the basis of human conscience and morality. Seventh there is a racial proof. It is based on a new sense of all human beings and is a way to prove on the basis that everyone on earth is aware of God and basically trying to serve it. It is the eighth happiness proof.

This means that humans on earth have a tendency to pursue basic happiness, and God is there for the pursuit and maintenance of this happiness. Finally, there is an ontological proof. This can be said to be inferring the concept through the existing God. In the Bible, it is generally revealed that God reveals Himself to Him (Psalm 76:1). It is God Himself who reveals Himself and manifests Himself through Jesus Christ. God has always allowed us to know and reveal Him to humans who want to know Him.

In Isaiah 6:9, "the knowledge of God is said to be full of the world," is that man has opened to God so that he may come to God's new knowledge. Thomas has given this point and has seen that we can approach God through various ways of demonstrating God. According to him, the reason of human being provides a basis for reaching the proof of the existence of God, and we can reason about God. Can we, as his words, know about God's cognition and deduce his existence?

This problem still has many theological theories and approaches today. God is transcendent but inherent, and at the same time reveals Himself to man through the Bible. Here we can look at God's active intrinsic and transcendent ministry.

GOD'S ACTIVE SELF-REVEALTION

We must think about the error that transcends human cognition and in addition, to God, who transcends human imagination and is in danger of being easily lost. This is the limit of human perception.

Human thinking is partial. Therefore, God's perception in the context of human marginal perception is imperfect. A man knows God partly. In other words, human reason confirms a partial awareness of God. Through the self-revelation of God approaching Scripture, man experiences God's perception of God Himself in the Bible, so that he will hear God's Word and know God. But even this experience is true within our own limits.

Knowing the object of God opens up the 'always the possibility' that allows God to reveal his revelation to man. 'Always Possible' is God's way of self-revelation. God does not stop the humans coming to Himself, knowing Himself, seeking for intelligence, but rather showing Himself to such humans, showing Him way and speaking through the Bible.

In the Old Testament, Adam and Eve eat the forbidden fruit God forbid. The fruit of not eating is the perfect law to control man of God. God's law has human freedom as long as it does not commit human beings outside God's law. But man breaks the law of God and falls into sin. The self-denial of the law of God has begun. Man finds the meaning of existence as a person through self-recognition before God as a human being in God's appointed garden. But self-acknowledgment denies self and negates the law of God so that self-acknowledgment brings to the limit of the recognition of human God with self-denial.

Human beings are separated from God and are now placed in the confusion of their own coming to know God. God commands these men to know God, but to the men who are blind to them, they kill the beast instead, clothes their skin, and shows God's 'possibilities' all the time. This is a demonstration of God's active self-revelation. The perception of God is that humans perceive God by themselves, but they should not regard God as a subject of inquiry or research. To analyze God as a subject for research is to be self-deprecating his own self-delusion.

We can approach God through 'always possibilities' in which God wants to speak to humans and come down to humans. Thomas's method of proving God's existence is not an approach to God's 'always possible' for man but an approach to God. This approach invites serious contradictions. In other words, the limit of human perception is that it can lead to a wrong approach to God. Self-depreciation caused by human corruption is the self-confidence of God through self-denial rather than complete recognition of God. If a man recognizes God in the state before the complete depravity, then perhaps the perception of God is accurate and certain.

However, such a new expression can lead to a flow of ideas into God's other conceptual concepts, not to speak God exactly. In other words, our perception of God is very partial.

There is a single oak tree here. This tree is over 500 years old. But the leaves of this tree are not of 500 years ago. Trees are made with new leaves as the year grows.

It is refreshing. In other words, the leaf that is harvested from this year's tree is the leaf from this year's growing tree, not the leaf that was limited to last year. Leaves grow according to the growth of the tree. At first, the leaves are those of the tiny child, and as the tree undergoes the corresponding growth process, the tree grows year by year, and the leaf corresponding to it grows. So is the perception of God. We are living the reality of supplying the necessary nutrients right now, and when the winter of life approaches, it is nothing but a flesh to leave everything away and leave.

But as the body of the tree is as it is, God is eternal and eternal from pre-creation to the time of God. We are seeds that have the growth potential to receive new power from God within the peak of God's time. We take off our outer garments and the leaves hold the new seeds and wait for the next moment. We have lived in God's 'possibilities' all the time. Through the active ministry of God, we go through the meaning of life before God through the birth of a new being. But it is a fragile body that can always be cut off by the wind. Leaves separate from the tree when the willingness to be attached to the tree is insufficient. If God does not have the will to exist, the human being is separated and alone.

It is self-denial without God's awareness. This possibility of self-denial also exists in man himself, and God's active revelation also coexists in the world.

Human is an incomplete other person and at the same time an independent self who is aware of God's self-revelation before God.

WHAT DO WE NEED TO BELIEVE IN GOD'S SELF-AWARENESS?

It is connected organic through existence. And because it has its own possibilities, it exists through its own way. God made this world. He ordered from the Word, and from the nothing to the being, from self-denial to self-awareness. Things did not exist before God made them.

However, the creation of God made self-denial possible by self-awareness, and the 'always possibility' of God's self-awareness gave the seed to the heart of man, so that even when the leaves fell and everything returned to nothing, he has opened the way of self-awareness for the new beginning. It is the holy plan of God, the sovereignty of God, and the providence of God.

The law of nature is made to dominate and sustain nature. And through the laws of nature, all human beings and all things come to establish their own basis of existence. God sets up, God preserves, and God works. Human beings live by living their own way of survival with the principles and rules God has set. Therefore, nature is the revelation of God, and God's revelation of that nature makes man have a moral nature and directs it to an ethical life.

Without such an idea, the human cannot stand as true beings. It does not mean that there is no human autonomy. In other words, human autonomy means autonomy from what God reveals. Human beings can never have autonomy without God. The autonomy itself is a deception of human self-denial.

The influence of the Enlightenment in the nineteenth century has begun to dominate the reason. Human beings here have found a basis to be free from the middle Ages and have begun to seek independence from God.

However, this autonomy is not the autonomy in the true sense, but the liberation from God. Man can not seek liberation from God himself. As long as self-denial exists, man cannot be independent of God and can never be free from God's recognition. Man's self-denial to God is merely to admit and acknowledge God. Human morality proves this. Humans call themselves moral.

The humans pursue moral one and hope for holiness. They want to protect themselves from uncleanness. This basic humanity of holiness is proof that man can not free himself from God. Humans have their own limitations. The first is a limitation from the physical. The body surrounds human beings. The body determines human identity. We can not do it freely. Freedom from the body is death. There exists human perception and reason exists.

In other words, the fact that we are in a physical body means that we can be accepted as a meaning of a being that lives in this world as a being with a body. Animals also have bodies. The plant also has a body. But their bodies are not recognized. Second, human beings are limits to spiritual things.

The recovery of spiritual things is only possible through the affirmation of God's approval. It is the holy intervention of God. God knows the limits of human spirituality. And man is hoping to restore his limits through the way God has given him.

Third, it is the intellectual limitations of a human being. Man is to know God through his own intellectual ways. Religious practice is an intellectual activity. Religion is what man made.

God's self-awareness is the realm of God that God only allows. Therefore, if human beings approach God with intellectual things, intellectuals create human beings' laws and make them religious. God is not interpreted in religious ideas. God opens his possibilities all the time, but it can be said that the answer to this is possible by solving human self-denial and approaching human perception of God.

The Incarnation, Jesus Christ

1. The fulfillment of God's promise
   Genesis 3:15 (the starting of Gospel)
   Isaiah 7:14; 9:6
   1) Christ is incarnate-in the human body, in the body of the virgin (conceived by the Holy Spirit, Isa. 7:14)
   2) The Son of God (Matthew 1:23)-The divinity of Christ
   (John 1:1; Romans 9:5, 1 Timothy 3:16,)
   3) The people of Israel, the sons of David
   (2 Samuel 7:16)
   4) The prophecy of being King
   (2 Samuel 7:4-17; Isa 9:7, Luke 1:32-33)

2. The Cross of Christ-opening the way of salvation
   (1 Corinthians 15:3; 1 Peter 2:24)
3. the resurrection of Christ-Jesus Christ's resurrection, objective evidence (Acts 1:3)
   1) The event giving us hope-the first fruit

2) Jesus' resurrected body-physical (Luke 24:42-43),
spiritual transformation (1 Corinthians 15:45)
3) Resurrection is believed through the Holy Spirit
   (Acts 1:7-8)

4. The ascension of Christ elf-indulgence (John 6:62)
"Then what if you were to see the Son of Man ascending to the place where he was?"
1) An important event linking Easter with Pentecost
2) Ascension means Jesus' ascension (exaltation).
Acts 2:33; Philippians 2:9
3) Sitting at the right hand of the throne of God (Ephesians 1:20).
4) Jesus ascended to be our high priest (Hebrews 4:14).

THE GOSPEL IN GENESIS

In Genesis, the fallen story of man comes out. Adam and Eve eat forbidden fruit which God would not eat. The fruit is the beginning of God's law for man, whom God has not permitted. Man first experiences isolation from God by breaking the law of God. Humans are diluted in value as dignity, and sin is in man. Through man's leaving from God's law, he brings murder and all sorts of sin to man. But to man who breaks the law of God, God comes in love.

That is to say, a man gives his labor all his life, and the woman gives her the labor of suffering which gives birth to a child. What is gained through labor is the price of God's punishment. The work of a man in society is accompanied by all the pain and suffering. Social life means economic life. The economic life began at this time.

Due to economic activities, human beings have poor and bad people's phenomenon, and human isolation and isolation from reality arise. Social conflicts are amplified and social problems arise. The pain of suffering has brought about the phenomenon of society today.

Next, the labor of the woman's conception opened her eyes about suffering. People who open their eyes to suffering have distorted all things and this phenomenon is prominent because of human birth continually.

God is aware of and confronts the confusion of the human society brought about by this human fall. Because God made man, he has a holy responsibility to man. That is, God's recovery of the fall of man began. And God says that he will crush your head and you will strike his heel. God opens the possibility of salvation to them by giving the gospel to fallen human beings.

PERSISTENCE OF GOD'S SALVATION MINISTRY

God opened the way for man through the primitive gospel.
To this end, God continues through his humans: Through Adam and Eve, through Seth, through Enoch, through Noah, and through Abraham, to the ministry of the redemption of God. God's ministry is through men.

It is not that men have opened it because there is no one as trustworthy as a human being because he is never perfect.

God's always-possible was planned and worked through man. God establishes faith and leads man in faith. Through Abel, Enoch, Noah, and Abraham. In addition, through the people of all faiths in the Old Testament, God's always possible is achieved.

Through the divine and holy ministry of God, God, as the subject of human history, desires to lead them. The Old Testament God is Almighty God, working as Elohim, Jehovah, Yahweh, and Adonai.

This name represents the divine authority. At the same time, God is represented by God, a personal being. God has his own messenger, works in human history, reveals himself, and opens the possibility of God's self-recognition to man.

In Genesis 22 God commands Abraham to sacrifice his prophet, Isaac. He walked with Isaac toward Mount Moriah without rejecting God's command. Isaac asks his father. "Where is the sacrifice to be given to the Father God?" Abraham replies that God will prepare for his son's words. Abraham obeys God's command. And God leaves with the Son with the conviction that everything will be ready. Abraham can see that he is thoroughly prepared for God's ministry. It does not mean that Abraham will put a sheep on the bush instead of Isaac. Whether God receives Isaac's offerings or not, invariably Abraham does not doubt God's work, but that he has given everything to God's sovereignty. As soon as Abraham is offering his Son as a sacrifice, the voice of God is heard, and Abraham hands the sword from his hand. Abraham passed the test of God and Abraham became God's acknowledged moment.

And instead of Isaac, God permits a sacrifice in a thicket and commands it to offer a burnt offering. Abraham calls it *Jehovah Jireh*:

Jehovah will provide. Through the process so far, we can tell about God's work as follows.

In other words, God wants to reveal his revelation to man and to interpret it together with human beings. Through his manifestation, God strongly desires that humans acknowledge God's appearance, clothe him, obey God's command and follow it. God can open the possibility of self-revelation to man constantly. It is Christ Jesus who opened the possibility of God's self-revelation. God sent Christ Jesus so that humans would believe in Jesus, receive Him, and accept Him. Jesus Christ is, in other words, God's self-manifestation.

SELF-MANIFESTATION OF CHRIST

God reveals Christ Jesus in many places through the Bible. This is God's self-imputation. Jewish religious leaders had to know God's self-assertion in this Word of God. But they did not know the voice of God through revelation through the word of God.

In Psalm, God said that He will establish the King of Israel in Zion, who is the universal and sovereign Son of God, who completes the ministry of salvation and the fact that God is worshiped through him. In addition, in relation to the ministry of Christ's salvation, Christ has revealed that He came as a savior and that He is the King of the universe. He is a descendant of David and is on this earth. It is the Son of David who works in this land to replace the ministry of salvation and creation that God accomplishes and to be completed as God. This fact becomes more certain when we go to the book of Prophet. The prophet Micah reveals that he is to be born in

Bethlehem, that he is the ruler of the universe, and that his body is born of the holy virgin. He tells himself that he has all the sufferings of man as a human being with God's attributes. Isaiah 53 speaks of accurate prophecy and reasoning about the Passion and suffering that he will go through.

He says that He came to this land to restore the price of the fallen self-denial because of man's sin and as the God of peace and holiness, grace and blessing.

Just as John the Baptist came to prepare the way of Jesus Christ, Jesus Christ came as a reserve to prepare the way of the kingdom of God to come.

CHRIST'S HUMANITY AND DIVINITY

Christ is God and man. Christ, God has worn the human body and manifested itself in the flesh.

That is, the perfect, omnipotent, infinite God accomplished His active revelation toward man through Jesus Christ. God has come beyond the limits of the human body to become human beings. It is an active intervention of human history through God's work.

Jesus Christ was conceived by the Holy Spirit in the body of the virgin. The incarnation of God is done. The fact that God has worn the body of human flesh has opened Him so that humans can see the existence of God close to them. The manifestation of God in the Old Testament is mainly through the prophets, through the tabernacle of God in the wilderness, and through the temple in the days of the monarchy of Israel. God's being was holiness itself.

The Old Testament God was in the midst of mankind, but he did not show himself entirely to human beings except for certain people. Therefore, it was a very unimaginable problem for the Jews to come down to this land with the human body of God, Yahweh God, Elohim.

The Jews rejected Jesus Christ. They had a doubt that how can a man like himself be God? Because of the Jewish thought of the Old Testament God, they did not see the true picture of the Messiah. Here we must make sense of the manifestation of Jesus Christ in the flesh. The fact that Jesus Christ came down to human beings with flesh. A through self-lowness can be seen as referring to the incarnated Jesus Christ.

There is a rich king here. He has riches and he is a man of honor and all power. No one can get close to him. People are only afraid of bowing their head before him. One day he saw where the poor people live and how they live. What would happen to a poor people if it were supposed to be ready in the months the king would come? Perhaps they will be busy first cleaning the house in which they live.

To greet the king, they will throw away their shabby clothes and change into new garments. In this way, they will be converted into totally different people, not their original appearance, and will welcome the king. The king would like to see their actual life, the well-organized ones. It is this concept that God has come to earth with the human body. Jesus Christ came to the earth to die on the cross for human sin.

Therefore, the image of Jesus Christ is never born rich with the appearance of a brilliant king. Jesus is the person who understands the condition of man better than anyone else. He came to this land to have the same body with us, to suffer with them, to mourn, to eat with us, to grow up with humans, to understand and love as well.

God's all-around possibility was completed through Jesus Christ. In every New Testament, Christ is called the Lord. In particular, Jesus speaks of his divinity through the parable of the owner of the vineyard in the Gospels. There is the owner of the vineyard. However, the servants of the vineyard act like the owners of the vineyard. Servants forget their identity, and those who have been sent by their master are beaten or killed by his own sons. Here the Son means Jesus Christ. That is, people who are sent to the Savior on this earth cannot recognize Jesus and take that life. Jesus Christ is speaking of this parable and wants to know that he is the Messiah who came down to this land as the Son of God. Jesus has done many miracles in the New Testament as the Son of God and the Lord who has put on the flesh of man.

Even to God's creative ministry, the Lord works and rebukes the sea to calm down, to walk on the water, and to revive the dead. And he proclaims forgiveness of sins to sinners and changes the concept of the Jews' law. Christ declares the commandments of the law in two ways.

To love God with all body, soul, and will, and then love your neighbor as your body. This is a demonstration of the fact that Jesus Christ has been working on this earth as a redeemer of God's law of the Old Testament and as the sole authority of God. Thus, Jesus can be said to be a person who is fulfilling his commandments, and who later turns to the cross to show people the way to come to God, the truth, and the life.

The fact that Christ has divinity confirms and assures him that he is doing in the ministry of the atonement as God. In order to live without sin, we need a flawless offering. This is the law and commandment that God has ordained to the people of Israel in the Old Testament. Because God has made it his own, God needs an eternal and perfect ransom to fulfill the Law at once, according to the law that He has set.

Therefore, knowing that the incarnate Christ is the most suitable person, it is incarnated as the Son of God, because he is to be safe without sin so that it is free from sin, and he gives himself to God as eternal atonement according to God's will. The sacrifice of Jesus on the cross can be seen as one of the proofs that He is God.

JESUS' DEATH ON THE CROSS

[The event of God's holy will]

God's holy will means restoration from the sins of man through the depravity and restoration to the order of the collapsed creation. Because of this holy will, God accomplishes His ministry and is given the sovereignty and power of God.

God's will is unchanged. To rebel against the will of God is to rebel against the Master. God's will is perfect. God's will is holy. God's will means the order for all disorder and the will of God means the recovery of the original will of his creation.

God opposes everything against his will. In the Old Testament, God disciplines the people who are beyond God's will.

And encourage the people through them to come back to God, and sometimes as shepherds lead the sheep. God wants the creation to return to Him. God plans and ministers so that the creatures can return to Him. Therefore, there can be no one who acts against these intentions of God.

Because God is the Almighty God who works in His own will, and plans and accomplishes it. The death of Christ's crucifixion is the decisive event of God's holy will. Christ clothes on the human body and came down to the earth. It is God's will that Christ came down to the earth, and God's will for ministry through Christ. God wants to accomplish perfection through Christ. Therefore, it can be said that the event planned by God is an event of the cross. The cross of Christ is the event of self-degradation and at the same time the event of the recovery.

In other words, the death of Christ's crucifixion can be said to be the decisive event of God's holy will. In return for the depravity toward God's human beings, humans go to the path of self-denial. God is incarnated as the Son of God for this human recovery and is sacrificed on the cross.

The cross is the most dramatic at the stage of the completion of the redemption of God, and ultimately accomplishes the work of God's redemption through the blood of Christ sprinkled on the altar of the cross.

The cross is the completion of God's always possible.

The cross is the completion of God's always possible, self-throwing, self-sacrifice, which makes a dramatic shift to human history. Jesus Christ obeyed God's will by giving up on the cross. It is fully revealed to God through the denial of physical bitterness and suffering as a human being. Jesus Christ confirms his personality by dying on the cross and completes it by witnessing to the people about the divinity. God wants to reveal Himself and open the way for humans to know Him.

The event of the cross can be said to be the most appropriate event for this God's purpose. There is no proper way to reveal Him as the cross. Only the cross has fully revealed his will to God's beings. God, through the sacrifice of Jesus Christ on the cross, wanted men to know the degree of punishment that humans should suffer from sin. Humans make the cruelty of the cross aware of the fear of the cost of sin. It is an event that shows the severity of the fallen humanity.

RESURRECTION OF JESUS

Christ died not only on the cross but also resurrected in the grave. This means that by self-assurance of death, God assures human life and permits eternal life. Resurrection means a free from death. Through resurrection, man is free from the power of death. Through the resurrection, a man recovers the nature of human existence. Jesus Christ is the first fruits of human beings who desire all resurrection. By Resurrection of Christ God is resurrecting to Humans is another of the events that show the divinity of Jesus Christ.

Through the resurrection it proved that Jesus Christ is the Son of God. Therefore, a person who believes and follows the event of the resurrection can be said to acknowledge Jesus as God and accept His whole life.

Without the resurrection, Christianity does not exist. "If Christ has not lived again, your faith will be in vain, and you will still be in sin (1 Corinthians 15:17)."

The resurrection of Christ brings about your identity to Christians. Thus, the resurrection of Jesus is proof of the life of Jesus as the basis for establishing full self-identity as a Christian and for Christians to await their resurrection and for the reason, they exist in the hope of the resurrection of Christ. Therefore, the resurrection as a Christian can be said to confirm and assure their salvation more firmly as a subject and self-identity.

Jesus resurrected both soul and body together. The event of Jesus' resurrection is a historical event corresponding to Jesus, as well as a present-day hopeful event transcending times and races. Through the resurrection of Jesus, people hope for resurrection, and through Jesus' resurrection, they seek their identity.

Through the resurrection of Jesus, people can be said to be born again, having self-affirmation, and having the meaning of Jesus' resurrection in response to God's ever-present possibility. In the words of God's ever-present possibility, it is God's possibilities. Likeness always corresponds to the attribute of God's love.

God gives opportunities to sinners and opens up the possibility of overcoming human self-denial. This is done through Jesus' resurrection.

Therefore, the resurrection of Jesus acts as a testimony to the resurrection of human as well as a testimony to the victory against the death. Jesus' resurrection is a great work that belongs to those who have the hope.

All of these personal events are all things of the Church, and they are evidence as historical facts about all of Christians.

JESUS HIMSELF IS A WITNESS

The resurrection of Jesus is a testament to people who want to be saved. It is also experienced by those who witnessed the resurrection. The resurrection of Jesus reveals that the Lord is alive that the grave is empty, that he appears to the disciples to show them the flesh and to be holy.

The evidence of the resurrection of Jesus Christ is that He is coming as a practical meaning to the resurrection, that His body should be accepted as a means of physical and spiritual change. The witness of the resurrection of Jesus is a self-affirmation of the self-denial of man's fallen by sin and means the overcoming of the physical limits through Christ Jesus and the witnessing of the glorified God himself.

The Apostle Paul expresses the resurrected body of Christ as a spiritual body to the resurrection of Jesus Christ.

Through the first fruits of Christ's resurrection, people hope for resurrection in Christ. Through the resurrection of the perfect Son of God, people recognize that the path to overcoming the limit of self-denial as human beings is open through Christ, hoping for the Lord and prepared as Christians on earth for the restoration of the perfect body and soul of resurrection.

The resurrection of Jesus is only a one-time event, but through His resurrection, the resurrection of Jesus has a universal and absolute meaning after the Pentecost event of the book of Act. In other words, Christ is resurrected and enters into the privilege of being a child of God through Christ. He who believes in the resurrection of Jesus will have eternal privilege as a child of God and will be able to see the perfect faith God has shown to Abraham in this world.

ASCENSION OF CHRIST

After his resurrection, Jesus met several disciples. On the way to Emmaus (Luke 24:13-35), in Jerusalem, in the Ten Disciples (Luke 24:36; John 20:19), and to the disciples with Thomas, He met with his disciples. For about 40 days after his resurrection from the dead, Jesus walked with his disciples, confirming and witnessing his resurrection.

After Jesus' resurrection, he did his last ministries of earth and he ascended. And then, when Pentecost came, the promised Holy Spirit descended. The ascension of Jesus is the whole process of the coming of the promised Holy Spirit. Jesus' ministry of resurrection, ascension, and descent of the Holy Spirit can be said to mean the work of the Holy Spirit, which the Lord has sent in the completion of His ministry to Christ. Christ was the incarnation of man as the Son of God. This is Christ's lowness. The lowness of Christ is reversed by the ascension of Christ. It implies the coming of Christ after the ascension of Christ. This is the culmination of God's work.

Christ ascends to give His disciples hope. And by making the disciples stronger in their bonds and strengthening the unity of the disciples, they will be at the forefront of preaching in the teaching of the Word of God.

PART I

CHAPTER 1

CHOSING FAITH AND UNBELIEF
Psalm 53:1-6 , Romans 1:17

Is the world divided into several views about God? The world is divided into two by the view of God. 'God lives' and 'no.' In other words, some people want to believe in God, and others do not want to believe in God. In other words, we can talk about 'God exists' and 'does not exist.' People are choosing one of two views about God's existence and non-existence. When we are not born, saying, "I firmly believe in God's existence." A child is a blank state of faith from the outset. You will be born without knowing anything.

Then, the children who meet the parents of the believer, through infancy, early childhood, and boyhood, gradually become aware of God through their parents and their surroundings (for example, going to church since childhood, evangelizing friends, etc.). Children who are unfamiliar with the environment will not be able to hear the gospel at all but will live as atheists even when they have a meeting about God's existence.

What I want to emphasize here is that no one is born, knowing that God's existence as a believer. Except for Jesus Christ, who was born as the Messiah, the Son of God, who was born at the time of his birth, a man was born in sinful nature and born to be unaware of God. Samuel also began to serve God in the temple when he was young, but when he was called by God, he was already raised and was able to discern the voice of his calling.

Therefore, except Jesus, all the people of the world are born of iniquity, and the knowledge and wisdom of knowing God are born blocked by sin. They are born in a disconnected state with God, are raised in faith through the parents of faith, and in the environment of various faiths, and are in a disconnected relationship with God until they are convicted and converted.

Those who break this state and become children of the Lord are those who are convinced of God's existence, those who deny God without ceasing to be disconnected, those who live according to their will are those who refuse to believe in God, In their own way, regardless of God's intention, they serve idols and live as unbelievers. Therefore, in the end, the world is divided into those who believe in God and those who do not.

THEN WHY DO PEOPLE REFUSE TO BELIEVE IN GOD?

There are a number of reasons.

First, because unbelievers believe in themselves. They rely more on their knowledge or experience. The English evangelical theologian McGrath said this: "The people of the world, so-called intellectuals, and of intellect do not need God." Intellectuals are those who have knowledge of themselves. They say that they have created culture and civilization on their own.

In fact, many of these classes come from Genesis. A criminal man uses his tools to create a culture. After Adam and Eve sinned, his naked body was ashamed and made clothes with leaves. The first creation of God creates a culture of clothing. And when building the

Tower of Babel, they also make civilizations, bake bricks, and set up buildings. They have learned how to think and live by themselves. The criminal is thoroughly scientific, rational, and philosophical. They were leading science, challenging Christianity with philosophy. They think that Christianity is a religion that is unscientific, irrational, and unrealistic, unsupported.

And we think that it is a religion that does not match up with the Christian era and it is only a story that is out of reality. In addition, there are many religions in the world.

So postmodernists' views say that there is salvation in other religions. Secondly, unbelievers want to find the cause of Christianity that society is not so evil and purified. In other words, the church did not do it properly.

And if God is alive, if society is not so evil, then we are going to cover the responsibility of society's absurdity and contradiction in Christianity.

Third, the mind becomes proud and does not believe in God. The heart is hardened. People constantly oppose God. Their hearts become hard as a stone and basically say against God, saying that they no longer need God in their life.

Finally, people seek the lust of the flesh, the lust of discerning, and the pride of life. It is so delightful to sin in the world because of its pleasures and refuses Christianity without being able to escape from the sweet temptations of sin.

WHAT ARE THE REASONS FOR THOSE WHO BELIEVE IN GOD?

Generally, those who want to believe in God are concerned about the world after death. People are interested in judgment, and they pay attention to eternal life and punishment. Many believers hope for heaven. And the whole fellowship with God in eternal heaven. Some people recognize the problem of their life and believe in God for recovering. Science does not explain where people come from and where they go. It can not explain the origins of humans.

However, the Bible answers. Other than the Creator God, we can know the origin of our humanity through the Bible. Therefore, one tries to believe in God. They can not find the ultimate meaning of life if people come from animals. The fact that it was created by God is seen more convincingly. The Word of God is exactly recorded.

The Bible is the Word of God. And the Bible is so wise that all our lives can be applied by the Word of God. Many people find the very foundation of faith in God through Jesus Christ.

The foundation of our faith is Jesus. Through the gospel of Jesus, people have faith. And through Jesus, we become children of God. Anyone who hears the gospel of His death and resurrection will believe in the holy God.

IS GOD THERE? ISN'T HE THERE?

We have to select everything on either of these. Your faith must choose one of these. Which one do you choose?

The French philosopher Pascal leaves the following famous words in his book Panse. "There is no way to prove our belief in God. However, our life is not harmed by the fact that God has lived all over the truth that I believe in. If our beliefs win, we will gain everything, and if we do, our lives will not lose anything, and we will live the most worthwhile life."

This means that it is much more beneficial to us to believe in God than to choose the faith of unbelief that we do not believe in God and to be with us now. It is very meaningful. Our faith is very personal. God is He who exists, regardless of our choice. God said to Moses, "I am who I am." God is God, who is interested in what we choose to do. The believers are delighted in putting everything in the presence of God, and there will be no harm to the saints who put their lives in charge of all things to God.

The wicked believe that God doesn't exist among them. By their being, they will not be able to escape eternal destruction, and while they are alive, they will be left to their own fleshly immorality and will live an unhappy life in their life.

WHAT IS THE POSITION OF OUR FAITH?

Christian doctrine is of God who we believe. We must find ourselves before God. We are creatures of God and are separated from God because of sin. Sin is blocked by God and us. The hurdle is an obstacle to knowing God. But God himself has removed the obstacle. He removed the disorder. We can go to God through Jesus.

Through Him, we are now all healed. God the Creator became our God and made us know the purpose and meaning of life. Anyone who meets the Lord comes out of the deep wandering of life. He says that our faith must come to the Lord. The belief that the Lord lives and is with us is testifying to God. Therefore, our faith must walk on everything that God is alive.

It is because there is never a loss to us. The Lord most desperately wants us to choose Him. Once we choose the Lord, He shows us that the choice is not wrong. The Lord himself proves that our choices are not a regrettable choice, and he gives us confidence.

"All that the Father gives me will come to me, and he who comes to me will never cast me out (John 6:37)." "For the LORD has rewarded me according to my righteousness, and has repaid me according to the cleanness of my hands. For I have kept the ways of the LORD, I have done evil, and have not departed from my God, and have not abandoned statutes before me (2 Samuel 22:21-23)."

[Meditations]

Why should we decide to believe in God?

+ You decided to put all of you in "God is there."
Then there is a reason why we must believe in this God. First, meditate on the following words.
(Genesis 1; Psalm 19; Romans 1 and 2)
+ We explain why God must be on four grounds:

First, all things in the world are causative. Second, the world is so subtle and rational that it is so scientific and rugged that it is hard to believe that it came about by chance. Third, humans did not happen accidentally. Fourth, it explains in detail how God lives in the Word.

+ What does it mean that all things in the world have a cause? (Psalm 19)

+ How does the created world prove God? (Job 38-41)

+ What does it mean that we are never an accidental being?

+ What does the Word testify about God? And what is needed to acknowledge God? (Hebrews 11)

CHAPTER 2

WHY SHOULD WE DECIDE TO BELIEVE IN GOD?
Isaiah 59:13-21

YOU HAVE DECIDED TO PUT ALL OF YOU IN 'GOD IS IN YOU.'

Then there is a reason why we must believe in this God.

First, meditate on the following words (Genesis 1; Psalm 19; Romans 1 and 2). Genesis 1:1: "In the beginning, God created the heavens and the earth." This is the first book of the Bible, in Volume 66, and the opening of the Word of God. Faith starts from believing that God created heaven and earth. If you do not believe in God's creation, then the whole of Christian doctrines, such as the depravity, Redemption, Resurrection, Second Coming, etc., will be destroyed.

It is the foundation of faith and faith in God. The Bible begins with creation and ends with the end (Revelation). The subject of creation is God, and the creation of the universe in the Word by the Word means the absolute power and sovereignty of God, and the world of all creation is arranged in the order in relation to the date of creation. Psalm 19: "The heavens declare the glory of God, and the firmament shows the work of his hands. God makes a covenant with the created world and man(creature). A covenant is a covenant with God. All the worlds of creation cannot be separated from God. God created the whole universe and made the man. Therefore, the meaning of my existence can be found through God, and I can find the answer only in God, even if I am born to live on this earth. God gives us revelation. Revelation is manifested in the general world (not just the created world, all creation worlds are evidence of God's existence) and special revelation(God's law, the fulfillment of God's promise through Jesus Christ) do.

Romans 1:2; "The righteousness of God appears in the gospel and leads to faith by faith, as it is written, the just shall live by faith." Paul defines the theme of the whole of Romans as the Gospel. God's righteousness is manifested in the gospel, which is the total conclusion of God's will to forgive the sins of mankind through the redemption of Jesus Christ and to make them children of God through the redemption of God. Therefore, those who hear the gospel will not be put to shame, and the saints will live in it.

In conclusion, we must believe in God because first, God created the heavens and the earth, and we were included in the creation. Second, God revealed Himself to reveal Himself, and all human beings are revealed naked before God's revelation.

Thirdly, because we already have the righteousness of God. God's righteousness is contained in the Gospel.

WE EXPLAIN THE REASONS WHY GOD MUST BE ON THE FOLLOWINGS FOUR GROUNDS.

We knew that there was a clear reason to believe in God. It is based on the clear fact that God is alive. God is alive and he has made all things. We have to trust God because God is there. How can you know that there is God? First of all, it is the very cause of everything. Second, all things prove that God is alive. That is, the world is so scientific and rational that it is so difficult to imagine that it came about by accident. Third, all things have a purpose. Fourth, the Word of God is witnessing this.

EVERYTHING IN THE WORLD HAS ITS CAUSES.

What does it mean? (Psalm 19)

Everything in the world is a cause. This is an etiologic method. All the things we are living in and encountered are not done themselves. It was possible because it was the cause. The world we live in must have consequences, and it is the cause that provides the results.

The world we live in, the universe exists. Why? It is possible because it has caused this world. In Hebrews 3:4, it says, "There is a man who builds every house.

He who made everything is God." Because God made it, there are all things in this world. People of unbelief do not accept it. They assert that all these things claim to be made by themselves. And it feels negative about the Christian faith. But which of the two is more convincing, because God created the world and believed that this world existed and that such a subtle, orderly world in which we live was created on its own? It is hardly convincing to say that it is made by itself, but it does not fit in an era that demands rational and reasonable things.

HOW DOES THE CREATED WORLD PROVE GOD?
(Job 38-41)

The created world in which we live demonstrates directly the existence of God. The creative world has a certain order, and according to the order, the entire universe is maintained and sustained. Even if there is a little confusion in the order, the order of creation collapses and accumulates in extreme confusion.

Nowadays, threatening the planet is a problem of 'warming.' It literally means that the earth is getting hot. The creation order is destroyed by the human God created. When the temperature of the earth raises a little, the weather changes everywhere in the world, and the imbalance of the ecosystem causes disaster to a human being. The original creation world should not be free from the order God has established.

God planned it, but an ignorant man challenges himself in order to cause disaster. When we see that the entire universe through the collapsing order is in utter confusion, it is the responsibility of the human being who can not see and manage God's creation world. The world created by God is a testament to the existence of God.

"For since the creation of the world God's invisible qualities his eternal power and divine nature have been clearly seen, being understood from what has been made, so that men are without excuse (Romans 1:20)."

People demand a more convenient life. The boat made to carry a lot of burdens makes us more aware of the providence of God's creation. People worry about how to load more. Thus, we found that the shape of the boat made between 0.21 and 0.30 in length and width is the safest and fastest and loads more. But this logic has been already in the world of creation. Biologists have found that fish can swim fast in the water, and they find that the ratio between the length and width of the fish is between 0.21 and 0.30. How can a fish have such a body? That is because it was created in the providence of God's creation.

Theories made by scholars advocating evolution are already considered hypotheses. Hypotheses are things that are not proven. In other words, evolution is a scientifically inexplicable theory that we have not accepted 120years ago.

WHAT DOES IT MEAN THAT WE NEVER AN ACCIDENTAL BEING? (Ecclesiastes 3:11)

This world is not just an accident. Likewise, we have no one who is born and lives by accidentally in the world.

The man has a relationship with God from birth. We are born with loss of God's image because we are conceived in the midst of sin. If you do not restore it because you are a sinner from the beginning, you can not but go to the path of destruction by receiving God's wrath.

For us, God has prepared the way through Jesus Christ. People do not have the special ability of animals. For example, it is not as strong as a lion, not as fast as a cheetah; it cannot fly as much as an eagle and does not have the correct vision. We can not smell as much as dogs, we cannot hear as well as the fox.

We can not swim like a fish. There is no special ability for many other animals in humans. But man is better than the animal. People never evolved from animals and do not return to animals after death.

Man is a distinct being in all creation. It is because God has given the man the image of God. He gave us a desire for holiness in our hearts, gave us a conscience, and allowed us to be religious. It is a person who can worship. Therefore, we were not born in this land by accidentally, but from the moment we were born on earth, we have to find God and are created to keep spiritual life in worship.

He who does not worship God is a man who has lost the meaning of existence and is out of his creation.

WHAT DOES THE WORD TESTIFY ABOUT GOD?

And what is needed to acknowledge God? (Hebrews 11)

The Bible says. "And without faith, it is impossible to please God, because anyone who comes to him must believe that he exists and that he rewards those who earnestly seek him (Hebrews 11:6)." The existence and creation of God is not a matter of analysis but a matter of faith. It is much more convincing to believe in a world of subtle creation.

The number of people who accept evolution has decreased, and now more people are accepting God's creation. They say that God is not such a person to discover in the laboratory, but on all creation (including all human beings therein) and wants to meet humans through faith.

There are not so many evidence that deny God's existence. Rather, there is more evidence of God's existence, and there are many things that are not explained in science that is explained in God's providence. The Word provides answers to all creation, not just my presence.

[Meditation] Truth Makes Us Free.

+ 'Choice' means that God has chosen us. To choose us, God created, believed, and gave us the truth.
What do you think about the truth?
+ Why do not many people believe in the truth?
(Ephesians 4:17-24; 2 Tim. 4:3-4)
+ What does the Bible say about truth?
(2 Timothy 2:15)
+ What is the way to know the truth? (John 14:6)
+ Why does truth make us free? (Ephesians 6:10-20)

CHAPTER 3

TRUTH MAKES US FREE.
2 Timothy 4: 3-4

'CHOICE' MEANS THAT GOD HAS CHOSEN US.

To choose us, God created, believed, and gave us the truth. What do you think about the truth?

The choice is not that we have chosen God, but the Creator of all things, and God, our Lord, has chosen and called us (John 15:16). Therefore, what we believe is God's great and wonderful providence and grace in our lives. God loves us and sends Him, and by His redeem we have been moved from a servant of sin to a servant of righteousness.

He who is in Jesus is no longer condemned. God made us, made us believe, and gave us truth. Here are some things you should be interested in. It is the word 'truth.' There are three prior meanings of truth. Firstly, it is a right and true sculpture related to the world affairs. It is true or false according to facts in logic. Secondly, it is recognized in philosophy when it is valid to anybody.

As an easy example, the universe has countless stars and other universes in the space. It cannot change in the future. It has already been decided, and so far the law has been kept. It is applied to anyone without changing, and it is the dictionary meaning of truth to always pursue what is right and what is true. However, if you look only at the lexical meaning, there is a problem.

It is the standard of interpretation of truth. For example, there have been many instances in which misunderstanding of truth has led to enormous disasters in human history. Hitler and his Nazi government believed that it was right to kill the Jews and assured them that there were no moral imperfections, killing 6 million people. That is, what he believes is truth, and he commands the Nazis to follow the truth. Clearly, the truth he has brought has brought great evil and misery to mankind. The truth may seem to be relative.

If I am right, it does not matter whether it is moral or immoral. It is a misinformed and applied false truth. We must focus on the criteria for interpreting the truth rather than on the content of the truth. What did you think about the truth? In Christianity, we place all standards on Jesus Christ in interpreting and applying truth. Jesus is the foundation of truth. It is the truth itself. God has chosen us to be able to triumph in the light of the truth of the gospel of Jesus Christ as the child of God.

WHY DO NOT MANY PEOPLE BELIEVE IN THE TRUTH?
(Ephesians 4:17-24 , 2 Tim. 4: 3-4)

This generation we live in is living in the flood of truth. In other words, I know the truth wrongly, and I do not know the exact meaning of the truth. People do not believe in absolute truth.

And I think that it is appropriate for an era in which we do not follow absolute and universal truths and do not believe, that is, we ask for rational and reasonable judgment.

People believe in themselves and trust everything in their knowledge, experience, and judgment. So I prefer the idea of postmodernism that relative truths rather than absolute truths exist anywhere. For example, there are many ways to reach the top of the mountain. The logic is that you can travel to various roads to reach the summit.

This means that the modern society in which we live is following the things that seem right to the eye. And they accept everything. If we don't harm ourselves, we don't care about anything else.

It's a way of thinking; it does not accept the absolute truth. Why? That is because if you have absolute truth, you have to follow that truth and your freedom is extremely limited.

It refuses to accept the truth, it hangs on the world moderately, and people refuse to accept the truth because it is easy for them to live without bumping into their thoughts and other people. "For the time will come when men will not put up with sound doctrine. Instead, to suit their own desires, they will gather around them a great number of teachers to say what their itching ears want to hear. They will turn their ears away from the truth and turn aside to myths (2 Tim 4:3,4).

WHAT DOES THE BIBLE SAY ABOUT TRUTH?
(2 Timothy 2:15)

The Bible does not teach a relative truth. The Bible speaks of absolute truth. God revealed to the truth through his Son. He said, "I am the way, the truth, and the life (John 14:6)." "When the Spirit of truth comes, he will guide you into all truth (John 16:13)." The apostle Paul and truth are in Jesus (Eph. 4:21).

In 1 Timothy 2:4, "God wants every man to be saved and to know the truth." All the standards for interpreting the truth are Jesus. In light of the truth that Jesus taught, God spoke clearly about the truth. When we stand before Jesus, we know what truth is.

We must understand rightly about the truth that God has given us, and not reject it unconditionally because we are different from our thoughts, but to be open to witnessing and knowing Jesus Christ, the perfection of God's revelation and truthfulness.

WHAT IS THE WAY TO KNOW THE TRUTH (John 14:6)?

Generally speaking of theology there are three ways to know the truth. One thing we want to say is that knowing this truth means knowing and realizing the truth revealed by God, the teaching of Jesus Christ. The first is our reason. Theologians used rational methods to know the truth and reach it. So we mobilized a rational way to demonstrate God's presence and faith in His ministry, especially Jesus Christ.

The use of the notion of the Trinity to explain God, Jesus, and the Holy Spirit was also a rational attempt to prove the existence of God. We can say that the method of proving God's existence was also attempted to explain God's way of existence by rational methods.

This was the way the medieval theologian Thomas Aquinas was influenced by Aristotle's philosophy. Not only are that, but all the theological interpretations and explanations that we have heard today also influenced by reason.

We can also see that participating in the study of God's Word and participating together has already been in a rational way to understand and study the Word. The second is faith. Some spiritual believers value faith more than reason. Only faith is needed to realize the truth. The words and doctrines that we often hear are those that come from a tradition of reformed faith.

Through the Reformation of Luther and Calvin, we have faith in God's Word. All that we now worship and serve is based on this Protestant tradition. In fact, human reason can make many mistakes. The wrong reason led to a great deal of misfortune in mankind, and misunderstanding and interpretation of God came about. They say that the way we can know God is from faith rather than reason. The third is an experience. People say that experience is important for the healing of repentance, grace and miraculous life to take place. We are standing right in the healing field of Jesus Christ, experiencing the Lord's healing touch on us.

As we experience, the Lord will know that he is truthful, and will have faith. We realize and feel the evidence that God is in our lives. So far we have learned about the way to the three truths. Then we can ask which of these three is more important. The most correct answer is that these three are balanced.

If we put too much emphasis on reason, we interpret the truth as distorted. There is a liberal theology that interprets the word distorted and denies the existence of God. And if you put too much emphasis on faith or experience, faith is likely to flow through mystical tendencies. Therefore, these three must be balanced. Sometimes we have to play a dialectic role in the truth about our beliefs (reason: knowing the correct doctrine and arguing). And we must confess God (faith). We must know God's grace and feel His life (experience). The Bible contains events that are difficult to understand reasonably. Faith and experience are important to accept the Lord's work, such as saving the dead, healing, and miracles taking place.

WHY DOES TRUTH MAKE US FREE (Ephesians 6:10-20)?

If we do not know the absolute truth, we will not know the meaning and purpose of our life.

In the end, we will end our life wandering around without knowing anything. These days our society denies the truth. If we do not stay in the truth which saying in the Bible, we do not know who we are, and the purpose of life as well. God showed us the truth. Why did he let us know what the truth is? We have made the truth known not to wander in the world anymore.

If we accept and acknowledge the eternal truth of Jesus, the wandering of our lives is over. It is no longer necessary to live in sin. From the condemnation of sin, true liberation will enjoy true freedom.

Zacchaeus did not know the purpose of life before meeting Him. He only knew that it was the only thing to live if he was treated as a sinner by collecting the taxes of their colleagues. When he met Jesus, who was true when he met the Lord, his long wandering ended. All the burdens of sin were released and he felt true freedom in the Lord. He was transformed into a new life. It is a new person. Jesus, the absolute truth, frees us. We find our true form lost in God and live in the thrill of living with God. We have already received the truth. Now we must bear witness to this truth, to live by believing and always experiencing the Lord of truth.

[Meditation] About God,

+ Who is God? (Acts 17:23-25; Hebrews 13)
+ What about God's character?
What character did God give us?
(Isa. 6:3; 1 John 4:7-9; Romans 3:23; Titus 3:5-7; Deuteronomy 8:16)
+ There is a character God does not share with us.
What is it? (Psalm 90: 2; Mal. 3: 6; Psalm 139: 7-10; Jer 17: 10; Job 42)
+ Why is it important to know about God in our faith?

Among the famous sayings of Dostoevsky are these words. "If people are convinced that God is not really there, then they try to do everything even doing the evil." The reason that people do their evil works but do not control themselves to some extent is that some consciousness about the God that "I am doing wrong things before him" suppresses their conscience. But once people are convinced that there is no God, imagine what will happen on earth. We can think of Dostoevsky's words this way. "If people feel that they are gods, they will not be able to do anything." It is dangerous to be sure that there is no God, but it is more dangerous to think that you are God. It is because the standard of judgment about everything is bound to be oneself. If I were a god, who would care? From then on, people will begin to the depravity.

CHAPTER 4

OUR FATHER, GOD
Acts 17:23-31

WHAT IS GOD LIKE? (Acts 17:23-25; Hebrews 13)

Someone was born in a very dark and unhappy environment. His father passed away early and his mother, who was alone, did all the hard work for him. She could not raise her child properly because of poor family circumstances.

To make matters worse, the child climbed a tree when he was very young and fell down to be a disability. Nobody looked at him. His mother also died of cancer when he became a young man. No one cares for this young man. He could not go out without someone's help. He curses God saying that there is no God in this world.

He poured all kinds of curses into his life every day. He despaired of his physical condition and lived in a grudge against the world. The embarrassment and shame is the image of the young man. He did not recognize God and rejected. This is the image of our human being who has left God. A man who has left God cannot get out of his way of sin and falls into the swamp of despair.

A sinned man curses God by rejecting God. This is what our past looks like. Before we accept God that we are personally our Savior and God, we are just like this young man who had to be forsaken with his fate. We can not deny it. British renowned Christian apologist C.S. Lewis left this remark.

"It does not mean that the glory of God is diminished by a man refusing to worship God, as a maniac does not lose the light because he is scribbling the word 'darkness' on the mental hospital solitary walls."

Sin makes people crazy. They crazy for a lifetime and go back to a bunch of dust in the end. They interpret God in their own life for the rest of their life.

Even if they do not, they can blame God. Why? It is because we are fundamentally unbelievers, in disobedience. Sin takes God and me away. It interprets God for its own comfort. If you interpret God in your own way, you will not be able to understand God's perfect will. God is the being whose character is not changed according to our thoughts. God is always God, regardless of our will.

Therefore, the greatest task in our faith and life is to know what God is like to us. Discovering God is the first gateway to the path of truth. God is outside the scope of our thoughts. We can never put God in our heads. We can not limit God to our thoughts. To find God in us, the scales in me have to be stripped off. The scales of sin must be stripped. The scales formed by our imagination or knowledge must be stripped off. God is transcending me.

God can always do in me, but He is working out for me and beyond me. Our God is the ruler of the universe. He is the Creator. Reign and creation are the rulers and the makers. It means that he is the ruler of me, and he still makes me. In order to know what I am before God and what God is for me, we need to know about God's character.

There are God's characters that can be shared with human beings or not.

WHAT IS GOD'S CHARACTER?

What character did God give us?

(Isa. 6:3; 1 John 4:7-9; Romans 3:23; Titus 3:5; Deuteronomy 8:16)

God was not created by anyone. God is eternally unchanging. James Packer defines this as "God does not perish forever." God is the one who is in Himself. No matter how sinners deny God's existence, it has nothing to do with God. The cry of such a sinner is nothing but a cry of a foolish man. God revealed Himself. And he has opened a way for people to know God. It is a bit of knowledge of God's character to humans.

The first is holy. The word holiness means far from sin. It means that you are not near to sin. God does not sin. The standard of holiness is God. God is holiness itself. A man has the heart to be holy. No one wants to dwell on sin. We hate sin. Why? Fundamentally, there is a desire for holiness. But human beings cannot be sanctified. We must resemble a holy God without sin.

If we do not resemble God, it is like giving up the path of holiness. Second is 'love.' There are three meanings of love in Greek: Eros (physical love), the love of Philos (emotional aspects such as parents, children, and friends) and Agape (love of God). God has given me three meanings of love.

Why did he do that? That is because love is the nature of God and the best personality. Love tolerates transgressions. All these aspects are included in human love. However, the greatest love among them is the love of Jesus Christ for the sinner, the love of the agape.

Third, it is mercy. Mercy also means long-suffering. We, humans, are sinners. The Bible says that the wages of sin are death(Romans 6:23). As a fundamental sinner, man is born in the world, and everybody is dead. No one lives in this world forever. God did not perish for us as sinners but prepared a way to escape. It is the prepared way of salvation through Jesus Christ.

This is God's mercy. In this world, God showed mercy to man so that no one would be condemned for sin and be judged for eternal punishment. God's mercy toward man has appeared as God's righteousness. Fourth is righteousness. Revelation 15:3 says, "The song of Moses the servant of God, the song of the Lamb, is great and wonderful, the Lord God Almighty. O king of the nations, thy way is righteous and true." According to the righteousness of God, everyone is condemned to receive the price of sin, which means that He has given us a way to live through Jesus because of His mercy.

By law, a person who commits a sin is sentenced to hundreds of years if not more than 200years. Where is the man who lives like that? This means that you will live in prison for life and die.

It is like a real death sentence. In the Bible, there is a person who ten thousand talents are owed. How much are ten thousand talents? One talent differs from one scholar to another, but some say it is 40thousand dollars and some say it is 100thousand dollars.

Ten thousand talents are astronomical amounts that can not be calculated. However, because of our sins, we owe the debt to God. In the tremendous debt that nobody can pay out of punishment for which no one can escape, God has forgiven everything with the grace of Jesus Christ. This is the righteousness of our God, and at the same time, mercy.

Finally, God is good. Our God is goodness itself. God did not create the world with evil motives. He always has a good heart for us. He will never throw away us. The one who lives in the days of the servants of the devil will eventually devastate everything.

Why? It is because the devil is evil. If you belong to the world, you can see and enjoy it on the outside, but it will be interesting, but eventually, you will be dragged to the devil, giving everything to the devil, and you will eventually have perished. There was a man who had a lot of money while he was taking medicines in a house in a certain village. He had a single son. There is no worry about eating and living. Because he was so rich, he had such a wealth that he could live and enjoy his life without having to work. By the way, as the son grows older and passes through puberty, the joy of the world begins to see. It seemed to him that he could live in the world with the riches.

The moment comes to the temptation of the devil. Let him live like that once. The devil tempted that I will guide you in a good way to enjoy the world.

When you have riches in your hands, you will enjoy all the pleasures of the world. The devil also says to have him require money from his father. The young man asks his father to return and share his legacy. However, he is severely insulted by his father. His heart is filled with an unbearable anger. He hears the voice of the devil, which should not be heard at the moment.

"Such a father is not a true father." He had a terrible idea and eventually, he drank alcohol and went home to kill a father. Later on, he regretted and regretted what he did, but coming back was the devil's ridiculous laugh. "I have done one thing today." The demons come a different path, but the devil is tempted to ruin one another, saying, "The devil has succeeded in destroying one another." If it is no longer worth the use of it, the devil has completely ruined one person.

The devil is like this. The nature is evil and should not be close. It is the way that leads us to the path of destruction. But our God is not. God's nature is good. He is perfect, and faithful toward us is endless. It is different from Satan, who draws us and feels the misery of sin and eventually throws it away. Our God always guides us in a good way. It is the way of life. Sometimes it is difficult, but if we do not lose God in our sight, but walk to the Lord and focus on Him, the good God will guide you in a good way.

[Meditation] Our Father, God

(The non-shared nature of God)

+ There is a character God does not share with us.
What is it? (Psalm 90:2; Mal. 3:6; Psalm 139:7-10; Jer 17:10; Job 42)
+ Why is it important to know about God in our faith?

CHAPTER 5

OUR FATHER, GOD
(God's Non-Communal Attributes)
Word: Psalm 99:1-9

THERE IS A CHARACTER GOD DOES NOT SHARE WITH US (Psalm 90:2; Mal. 3:6; Psalm 139:7-10; Jer 17:10; Job 42).

God understands us as human beings better than anyone else. Why does God only understand me? It is because we have the character of God in us. God knows us well because the nature of God is in me.

There are words that you write well. "Yes, I know your heart. I know it because I have experienced it once. How sad is it? God has the same mind toward us." He has more than that. Because God has given us character, we can get real comfort from God. And God alone is the one who solves all our problems. Why? This is because God has a character that God does not impart to man.

Because of the character God gave us, God knows us well, but because of his character, which is not shared with us, God knows and resolves all our problems and is among us as our God. The character that God does not share is the character possessed by God alone. First, it is 'eternal.' God is eternal.

You do not have a beginning or an end. Our God has always existed. And it continues to exist in the future. Man is not eternal. Everyone is born and dies after living in the Bible. The number of years is 70, and if it is strong, it is 80. Few people live for 100 years. All human beings are born to die. There is no one but Jesus Christ in this world who transcends death. God is eternal. Man gains eternal life through Jesus Christ. Those who receive the resurrection life will have eternal life. The wicked are not.

They are in eternal judgment because of sin. They will live in suffering from eternal punishment. Eternal life and immortality are given to us.

But the important thing is that once you are born as a human being, everyone will die and you will be waiting for God's judgment after that. It is because we are finite beings. Man can never be ahead of God. It is impossible to say that human beings become gods (in some religions such claims). Humans are not gods. Only God is eternal. We stand before that eternal God.

Second, our God is immutable. The word immutable means that it does not change. God has never changed and will never change.

The nature of our God is immutable. Like Hebrews 13:8, it is the same yesterday, today, and forever. All the world changes. We humans also change. As we are born, we look and grow while we grow old. Everything in the world changes. No one can stop change.

Our human being in the flesh continues to change. The mind also changes. Easily liked and easily bored. It is like a whim of youth. The character of our God does not change. The mind toward us does not change either. He is with us as one who does not change as the eternal. "I am the Lord who does not change (Mal 3:6)." Third, God is everywhere (omnipresent). The personality of God to talk about is omnipresent, omniscience, and omnipotent. These are the omnipresence, omniscience, omnipotence, omni- prefix, and so on. The word 'Omni' is infinite.

There is no end. Ubiquitous means that God is infinitely everywhere. Wherever we go, where we are, inside and outside of us, our God exists at the same time. If I go to church and sit down, God is there, even if I meet a friend, and he is there, even in the midst of my family. We can not deny God's omnipresence. God is with me where I am. He is the Holy Spirit. He sees all of me and knows my heart and my thoughts. "Wherever I am, you are with me, as I say to you," I will go to the valley of the shadow of death, but I will not fear the enemy, and the Lord will redeem me with a staff. Those who know God's omnipresence are those who walk with Him.

He who does not know God's companions is in a place where he is. He is a doubter. Therefore, they do not walk before God, but in unbelief. It is unbelief to know that there is no a ubiquitous God and to do what he wants to do. While the Israelites were living in the wilderness, God was always with them in the clouds and in the pillar of fire everywhere they went.

But the people did not know it and continued to sin. Thus, if we do not know God's omnipresence, we too can commit sin.

Fourth, God is omnipresent. He knows everything. Psalm 139:4 says, "Jehovah, there is none that does not know the words of my tongue." God is counting not only our past but also the present and the future. Nothing can be hidden from God. Everything is revealed before God. Moody, a global revivalist, had a friend. Together they worked hard in the ministry of the gospel. He was a friend who made Moody, and he was widely used before God. One day, he found a scripture that encouraged Moody to gain strength when he was struggling with a ministry. He also received great grace and comfort through scripture.

"I am not ashamed because the Lord GOD helped me, and I have strengthened my face like a flint, and I know that I will not be put to shame (Isaiah 50:7)." God is the one who helps us. He can help because he knows us well. Because God knows everything we judge, decide, and act on our own, God helps us in knowing that we will be weak and wrong. Therefore, those who believe in God faithfully turn their paths. For the one who knows my way is a God who is a wholly omnipotent.

Fifth, God is Almighty. God knows everything and is able to do everything. That is what God wants. God is Almighty. He gives life to the dead, gives eternal life, heals the sick, forgives sinners, creates and controls the heavens and the earth, and puts all things under the feet of the universe.

In Job 42:2, He says, "You are indifferent, and no matter what you do." If God wants to run it, it will be done. What does it mean to entrust all of our events to Jehovah? God is Omnipotent, so if you leave all of us to Him, He will lead you. God is our master and guarantor of our lives, so he works. But nothing will happen to those who do not believe. To those who believe in God, God is joined with great power. A Chinese young man came to Hudson Taylor, Chinese missionary. "How many years does it take to become a saint?"

Then Taylor says, "How long does it take to light the lamp?" "Just as soon as you put the fire on it, the lamp will light up." "Right. That's it. Just as light burns on the lamp, if God holds my hand, I will be captured by the power of God, and new life will be burned in me, and I will be held captive by the power of God."

Because God is Almighty, He gives victory to anyone who relies on God and goes with him. I hope to hold the hand of God's power in times of difficulty. Almighty God will help us.

WHY IS IT IMPORTANT TO KNOW ABOUT GOD IN OUR FAITH?

All that we are born and believe in God is possible because God is. Because God created the world, he made a man, so we exist. I was born of a parent, but the reason I was born is that I am born and grow because God has already made this world so. Therefore, God is the master and the master of the entire universe.

Because God has done it, we are living in the providence of God. For this reason, we must know God. I must come to know that I am standing by, not by chance, but by leading in God's wonderful creation plan. We need to know God. We must believe. Our life is not over yet until we go to God's house.

What have we lived in so far? We look back on our life. At that moment the voice of the Holy Spirit is heard. "Your welcome has not even begun in the kingdom of God." The welcoming ceremony of our Heaven cannot be compared with that of the earth. We have not arrived at an eternal house yet. Until we come to that day, we must serve God diligently.

[Meditation] God's Plan and Reign

+ What does the Bible say about God's creation and governance? (Psalm 47;97)
+ In what way is the word 'scheduled' recorded in the dictionary?
+ What does the word God's plan mean? (Psalm 93)
+ Let's think about God's reign.

CHAPTER 6

GOD'S PLAN AND REIGN
Psalm 47:1-9

WHAT DOES THE BIBLE SAY ABOUT GOD'S CREATION AND GOVERNANCE? (Psalm 47;97)

The Christian doctrine explains the creation of God using Latin. The creation of God is generally defined in Latin as ex nihilo. Here 'ex' means 'from.' And nihilo means 'nothing.' In other words, God says, "He created the heavens and the earth from nothing."

Therefore, all the sources of the world come from God. God is the foundation of creation and the subject. It is a word that transcends our human understanding ability.

In Genesis 1 God does not scientifically explain creation. It is just that God made the world. What does this mean? Whether you understand it with reason or do not understand it, God has created it, and our human origin has come out only from Him. It is not that he made things using materials, but in the Bible, he built the world through the Word, and he says that he made a man by using the earth already made.

So when a man dies, his body returns to earth created by God. And it will be until the resurrection of the body. The important thing is that God created it, and we are created beings in the providence of the Creator God. How did God make the world?

First, he created the world beautifully. Sometimes we see pictures of the beautiful earth in photographs and TV. The outer space of the universe is so beautiful. When you look at the shape of the entire world, you are once again amazed by the beautiful world. The world we live in is the extreme of beauty.

Second, God is transcending us. When we look at the character that God does not share with us, we are amazed at God's greatness and omnipotence. We must not judge or preach the God who transcends us beyond our knowledge of short human knowledge.

Third, God created and gave the order to the whole creation, making it as regular as a sophisticated machine. The world we live in is kept in order so that we think it is a great work made by someone rather than being created by chance.

Fourth, God has made and sustained. Once a person makes a sophisticated machine, he will not let it go. Attach a technician to keep the machine working without failures. When God makes the world, he is in direct intervention in the providence of God.

The problem is that we desperately want to destroy the order of creation, disregarding the providence and dominion of God, as though these wonderful technicians are in us, but they are broken down by leaving the machines to those who are not skilled in machinery.

This is because of human sinfulness. A sinful man does not acknowledge God. It is arrogant in itself, ignoring God's creation order and handling it in an intricate manner.

IN WHAT WAY IS THE WORD 'SCHEDULED' RECORDED IN THE DICTIONARY?

'Scheduled' is a very important concept in Christian doctrine. We must think of the word 'to be' and 'the whole grace of God' together. The preliminary meaning of the appointment is to "predict what will happen in the future." In the Bible, we say that God created and ruled the earth. And the will of God sustains and leads all these created worlds.

It is God's plan that God will direct, and that the whole will of God will influence all the created worlds. This corresponds to God's entire grace. God has planned, created, ruled over all human beings, and God continue to plan and do it in the future. We are people in God's plan. It is the whole grace of God for the created world, and we are those who receive the grace of this God.

WHAT DOES THE WORD 'GOD'S PLAN MEAN? (Psalm 93)

In 1643, 159 theologians gathered at the Westminster Church in England. There was a very special meeting there.
They gathered to establish all the worship, political doctrine, and theology of the Church in England, where they adopted the Westminster Catechism.

The Presbyterian has adopted this Westminster Catechism as an apostle and confession of faith. Our church also baptizes before receiving baptism and receives and answers baptism based on all the

Westminster Catechism. That is a very important confession. In this confession, we define God's plan in this way.

From eternity God established all things to happen freely and unchangeable according to his wisdom and holy plan through his own will (Eph. 1:1; Romans 11:33).

In order to manifest his glory by the economy of God, some of mankind and angels are eternal life, and some have been pre-empted into eternal death.

Those who are scheduled for life have chosen Christ in Christ, according to eternal, unchanging purpose, secret plan, and good pleasure, according to his will, before God has already laid the foundation of this world.

Not in their faith, in good deeds, or in the final deliverance in them or in other creatures, which may be the cause of the decision? Everything is chosen to praise God's glorious grace.

Therefore, the elect is actually called to come to faith through the Holy Spirit and is redeemed in Christ, and works in time. They are also protected by the power of Christ until they become righteous, become children of God, sanctified, and are saved through faith. God has neither mercy nor good will, as he pleased, to those who were not elected according to an immeasurable plan of his own will.

He was forgiving, embarrassed, angry with their sins, and glad to praise his glorious righteousness for the glory of God's absolute power over all creation. The planned doctrine, which is sealed in a deep mystery, must be treated with special discretion and care.

By doing so, we can know the will of God as revealed in His Word and trust each eternal choice. Therefore, this doctrine causes the praise, honor, and longing for God. Not only that, but also humility, diligence, and unlimited comfort to all those who genuinely obey the gospel. To those who believe, we give them the confidence of God's guidance and give them an opportunity to receive God's mercy.

LET'S THINK ABOUT GOD'S REIGN.

There is something common to people with unbelief. They can not believe many of the miracles and articles in the Bible. How can the red sea be divided, the water comes out of the rocks, the big fish that can be swallowed up, the dead can survive, and the castle can collapse even though it has been circumnavigated seven times? And so on, who do not believe in miracles and articles from the Bible?

So they simply give questions to God, a God who is hard to believe, and the Christians as irrational people.

Furthermore, it is even more unbelievable in Jesus' death and resurrection of the cross, the presence of the Holy Spirit, and the faith of the Second Coming. But as we walked personally in the Lord, believing in the living God, and walking in the path of ministers, we knew how foolish our thoughts were before we believed in the past, Jesus. God is never subordinate to human reason.

God is beyond human beings and transcends. So he is God. Because God created the world and made human beings, He is able to work beyond creation and humanity. The Creator God raises and calms the winds, and teaches the sea, and leads all creatures. A child is playing with mud and playing at will.

They make mountains, people, and animals. And they crack it again. Why? Because the master of the clay is the child. God does the same. Since the master of the created world is God, God guides us in his own way and works with power. Because of these miracles and reigns of God, all Christians who serve God as the sovereign will have a desire for victory. Because God is infinite, finite humans can not deny God's work. Westminster it is also clear in doctrine.

God, the great Creator of all things, is to be praised for His wisdom, for power, for righteousness, for the glory of goodness and mercy, and for the wisest and holy providence He protects, directs, disposes, and governs all creatures, actions, and materials from the greatest to the smallest.

And in the Confession of Faith, the Presbyterian Church, God's providence does fulfill his purpose of creation It refers to preserving, controlling, and leading all things created for them. God uses natural law, all creatures, human reason and conscience according to his providence, but by his righteousness, wisdom, power, and love, he fulfills his eternal purpose of creation. But the most righteous and good God does not make or acknowledge sin. God is the Absolute, the Creator of all things, and does not allow other divine beings.

All beings that are made of him must believe and worship the LORD God as the Absolute, and therefore we do not recognize the redemptive value of all religions that serve other gods.

[Meditation] What Is Jesus?

+ Let's imagine and talk about Jesus' appearance.

+ What is the character of Jesus?
(Luke 1:35, Colossians 2:9, Romans 9:5, Romans 1:3-4)
+ How can we express Jesus' identity?
(Philippians 2:5-8)
+ Jesus was born of a virgin with the power of the Holy Spirit, and had no sin.
(Hebrews 2:14, 16-17, 4:15) (Luke 1:27, 31, 35, Galatians 4: 4)

CHAPTER 7

WHO IS JESUS?
Hebrews 4:14-16

LET'S IMAGINE AND TALK ABOUT JESUS' APPEARANCE.

When people usually ask to imagine the appearance of Jesus, they usually look like a white person, thinking of blond hair, blue eyes, big tallness, and a stiff nose. This is the appearance of Jesus who thought it from the white people's point of view. The Gospel does not mention Jesus' appearance.

One thing we can see is that Jesus was born in a Jewish society at the time and would have had the appearance of a Jew. Looking at the Jewish appearance of the Palestinian area, the skin is yellowish brown, with black hair, brown eyes, and nose with hooks. And most of the Jews cultivated their black hair long.

Jesus used Arama at the time and this Aramaic would have spoken in the Northern accent because he grew up in Galilee as a branch of the Hebrew dialect. The Jews often wore underwear and a sandal on their sleeveless underwear, and they always carry wands.

By the lifestyle of the time, Jesus' appearance can make such a guess. Unlike our imagined whites, black ones, and yellow men, they would have the physical characteristics of the Jews.

Jesus' appearance is not that important. The important thing is that Jesus came from before the creation and came to earth to fulfill God's will. He is the Lord of the Holy Trinity, who belongs to God the Father and is not under God the Father because he belongs, but the Father, the Son, and the Holy Spirit are all equal persons and substances are different. Trinity will explain: He is our perfect Savior. Jesus came down to among us because of the work for the salvation.

WHAT IS THE CHARACTER OF JESUS?
(Luke 1:35, Colossians 2:9, Romans 9:5, Romans 1:3-4)

Jesus had the full personality of God, and at the same time, he had the character of perfect humanity. Jesus did not abandon the character of God even when he was born in human form on earth. He became the body of the Word. That is, God became human. Among the heretics, there were many heresies denying the human personality of Jesus. In other words, they asserted that Jesus claims to be God, but not human.

If Jesus is God and not a man, then the redeeming of Jesus is meaningless, and our salvation is in vain. Jesus is God. God has become a human being, a sacrifice, the Lamb of God, and he have redeemed human sins. Early Church leaders proclaimed in 451 A.D. the Chalcedon Council that Jesus became a perfect human being, a perfect God, and a savior for sin.

Thus, two perfect and unique natures-divinity and humanity can not be united, altered, mixed, or confused in an unbreakable person. He is a true person, Christ, and the only mediator between God and man(Luke 1: 35; Colossians 2:9; Romans 1:3-4).

WHAT CAN WE DO TO EXPRESS JESUS' IDENTITY (Philippians 2:5-8)?

We live with our identity in the world as we grow. We live by the status of a student, disciples, etc., as a teacher, as a clergyman, as a civil servant, as parents and so on. This status tells what the person should be like. To express the identity of Jesus, we must know the word 'kenosis.' This kenosis comes from Philippians 2:5-8.

This is the heart of Christ Jesus which is in you. He does not consider himself to be the body of God or equivalent to God, but instead of being a self-emancipated servant, he has become like people, He humbled himself, and was subject to death, for he died on the cross.

It is the kenosis that abandons one's identity and empties it. In fact, it is easy to empty yourself from a low position. The higher your status, the more difficult it is to down yourself. In fact, Jesus is the God who created the heavens and the earth. He is the power over the whole universe. The God has evolved from his identity and has become like the people with the shape of the servant. This grace is an amazing grace. No matter how low or lowly we are, we will appreciate any lowering when we think about Jesus.

Jesus' Kenosis:

+ Servant: Jesus came as a humble servant (Mark 10:45).
He came to serve as a servant in spite of all authority.

+ Being human: Jesus did not come in the form of an angel. Jesus, the God, has come to have human appearance through the human body.
+ Self-deprecation: in the English Bible, self-denouncing means "making you a non-existent person." He who has perfect divinity has come down with a body and humans himself.

Jesus had divine attributes. He is the owner of all things. He raised the sick, he became the master of all things, and he did great wonders and miracles. It is also evidence that Jesus is God. But Jesus also revealed his divine attributes.

He felt the same pain we felt when he was in a human body, he was sad when we were sad; comforted when we comforted and laughed when we were happy. When he was suffering from being crucified, Jesus did not do so, even though he had a troop of the angel which could take away the pain and punish the soldiers who crucified him. Why? This is the secret of Jesus' Kenosis.

It is all about the will of God. He has lowered himself and obeyed the will of God, becoming a man, and accomplishing the ministry of redemption.

JESUS WAS BORN OF A VIRGIN BY THE POWER OF THE HOLY SPIRIT AND DID NOT HAVE SIN.
(Hebrews 2:14, 16-17, 4:15) (Luke 1:27, 31, 35, Galatians 4: 4)

He was wearing the body of a man when the time came. He had all the fundamental elements of man that came out of it, but he did not have sin. He was conceived by the Virgin Mary in the power of the Holy Spirit and born in the body of the woman.

We humans have fallen because of original sin. Because we have fallen, we can not but sin. But Jesus is different. Jesus was tempted by Satan in the wilderness, but he did not fall because of it. That is why Jesus lived a sinless life. Because He was born without sin, He has enough Savior to redeem our sins. Jesus Christ was God, but the ones, who forgave our relationship with God and forgive our sins, and to restore us to the sons of God, Jesus, the sinless man, became a sacrifice.

If we do not believe Jesus was born and we will eventually have the same consequence of not believing the Bible, we lose a true guide who will restore us to the children of God.

The Lord Jesus fully satisfies the righteousness of his Father by submitting himself to God as a sacrifice through perfect obedience and the eternal Holy Spirit, not only for reconciliation He has obtained an eternal inheritance from heaven.

[Meditation] What did Jesus teach and work?

+ What did Jesus come and teach on this earth?
(Romans 6:23; Matthew 5:7; Matthew 22:37,38)
+ What position did Jesus have?
(Isa 42:1; Acts 3:22; Heb 5:5-6)
+ Let's consider the following of what Jesus did.
Transition, Sermon, Life, Salvation, Intermission

CHAPTER 8

WHAT JESUS TAUGHT AND DID
Acts 3:22-26

WHAT DID JESUS COME AND TEACH ON THIS EARTH?
(Romans 6:23; Matthew 5:7; Matthew 22:37, 38)

First, Jesus came to this place and taught people about salvation. A man was separated from God because of sin. We have chosen a way not to serve God. Jesus came to reconcile human beings with God. Meaning reconciliation means that Christians are saved and become children of God. A man without God has lost his way. We have lost the purpose of life.

Where did we come from and what should we live for? We have lost our complete goal. To believe in Jesus Christ and become a child of God is to discover the goal of our lost life and the purpose of life.

The merit of salvation belongs to Jesus, and the grace and blessings of salvation are what humans enjoy (Romans 10:10).

"Behold, I stand at the door and knock; if anyone hears my voice and opens the door, I will come into him, and eat with him, and he will eat with me (Revelation 3:20)." Second, Jesus taught about inner blessings. It is the outwardness that is the most disturbing of our salvation. Outward righteousness cannot be saved. Good deeds, morals, religious zeal, and asceticism have nothing to do with salvation.

If it goes in the wrong direction, it becomes a hypocritical life of faith. Jesus linked these dangers with the hypocrisy of the Pharisees and scribes. They lived in a formal, outward appearance. Jesus said that inner blessings are more important than these external ones.

He did these curses against the Pharisees, but he had eight blessings to those of true faith.

"Those who are poor in spirit; Those who are in heaven, Those who are mourning; Those who are comforted, Those who are meek; Those who take the earth as a corporation and do righteousness; Gain satisfaction with God; who sees God, who makes peace; who becomes a child of God; who and loving our neighbors is afflicted possesses heaven." Third, the greatest thing Jesus taught is love. This is the fulfillment of the law of loving God (Matthew 22:37, 38).

It is this also that the Apostle John also loves God, that we keep His Word; Commandment (1 John 5:3). If we love God with a sincere heart, not outwardly in love with God, not in a hypocritical attitude, our love will appear in loving God and loving our neighbors.

Jesus not only showed the love of God personally but showed us the best love of God so that we can not measure the height, depth, length, and width of God's love for man. It is that God, who is God, has given himself to us in order to become a human being in the form of a servant and love our human being. It is the ultimate in love, the noblest and important truth that the Lord has taught.

Often there is something we can easily misunderstand, that love is emotional. Love among men and women physically, love between parents and children, and friendship among friends can be emotional.

But God's love for man is never emotional. It is not emotional that we love God. It is obedience. Just as Jesus loved humankind and obeyed God's will, if we also love God, we must be in a position of obedience toward God in our lives.

WHAT POSITION DID JESUS HAVE? (Isa 42:1; Acts 3:22; Heb 5:5-6)

Jesus' first position is a mediator (John 3:16).

It is the mediator between God and man. This means that we cannot go to God without going through Jesus. Second, Jesus is a prophet (Acts 3:22). As in Colossians 2:3, He is full of wisdom and knowledge as the great prophet who mentioned in the Bible. It is the prophet of the truth. He is filled with gifts and truths, and he is not lacking in the judgment of the prophets.

Third, Jesus is the High Priest (Heb 5:5, 6). The priest of the Old Testament is the one who administers the sacrifice. As a surrogate of God, he served the sacrifice instead and played a role in connecting people with God. Similar to these meanings, Jesus is a priest, but a high priest with a deeper meaning than that. Jesus opened the way of the Lamb of God so that anyone could depend on His name and way to go to God. Fourth, Jesus is king (Psalm 2:6).

The king is the power. Jesus is the king of not only the world but the power of the whole universe. He is the King of Kings and the Head of the Church. Those who are under the power of the King, Jesus, will receive His eternal reign and guidance. Fifth, Jesus is the Head and Savior of the Church (Eph. 5:23). Sixth, Jesus becomes the heir of all things (Hebrews 1:2), and the seventh becomes the Judge (Acts 17:31).

LET US CONSIDER THE FOLLOWING OF WHAT JESUS DID.

Transition, Sermon, Life, Salvation, Intermission

Jesus came to this land and showed many miracles and signs. He opened the eyes of the blind and opened the ears and mouths of the impaired. He calmed the storm and healed the various sick people. He saved the dead. He forgave the sins of sinners and healed the sick with a heart. He fed five thousand, four thousand, and cast out demons. He has done a lot of things. There were always miracles and signs in the way of Jesus.

This shows that Jesus is the omnipotent God. Why did he do it? Because he had a compassion for people in the pitiful life of groaning in sin and wandering in pain. He did this to make Himself known as the Savior. Many miracles appear to those who are merciful today, who are the sons of God, and who want to believe primarily in salvation. Jesus ministered to the work of witnessing the Word.

He preached to the Jewish religious leaders (Pharisee, Sadducees) and preached to the people.

Through the preaching of the Word, many people have returned to Him through the Word of God, which is the truth of God. The Word ministry is an indispensable work of the Lord's ministry. Jesus preached and showed himself as a life. He personally practiced it in his life. He practiced love.

He contacted sinners, forgave them, and made them children of God. And Jesus chose the twelve disciples, the seventy disciples, and did intensive training of them. He has set up disciples. Today, the disciples of the ministry of the Word become disciples of the Lord. The disciples who are united in word and life can be called the true Lord of the Lord. To be a Christian like this is to become a disciple of the Lord. And it means that we must follow the way that the Lord has gone and follow him like his disciples.

Jesus fulfilled the way of salvation for all believers. Salvation is the power of believers. For those who do not believe, and to judgment. "But we preach Christ crucified: a stumbling block to Jews and foolishness to Gentiles, but to those whom God has called, both Jews and Greeks, Christ the power of God and the wisdom of God (1 Corinthians 1:23, 24)."

Jesus is interceding for us and praying for us. God continually forgives the sins of the justified." In these cases, they can not see the light of God until they lower themselves, confess their sins, seek forgiveness, and renew faith and repentance. In Luke 22:31, 32, Jesus prayed that our faith would not fail. This means that Jesus is still working for us. It means that Jesus prayed to God for us. But they are never abandoned, but are sealed in the day of redemption, and are promised as the successors of one salvation.

[Meditation] Who is the Holy Spirit God?

+ Let's learn about the personality of the Holy Spirit
(1 Corinthians 2:10, 11; Ephesians 4:30; 1Corinthians 12:11)

+ Let us know what the Holy Spirit is doing as a person
(Romans 8:26; Acts 3:39; John 14:26; John 16:13)
+ What character does the Holy Spirit prove to be God? (Heb 9:14; 1 Corinthians 2:10, 11; Psalm 139:7; Gen. 1:2; Luke 1:35; John 3:8
+The Holy Spirit God mentioned in the Westminster Confession of Faith

CHAPTER 9

WHO IS THE HOLY SPIRIT GOD?
1 Corinthians 2: 10-13

HOLY SPIRIT, LET'S LEARN ABOUT GOD'S PERSONALITY
(1 Corinthians 2:10, 11; Ephesians 4:30; 1 Corinthians 12:11)

Gravity refers to the force that the Earth draws all objects in the direction of the center. It is called the gravitational force, that is, the gravitational pulling force between the earth and other objects and the centrifugal force caused by the earth's rotation.

No one knew the principle until this principle was discovered by Newton. People just thought that only the apple falls off the tree. It was captivated by the simple idea of falling leaves. Before gravity has been found, gravity has been used as an invisible principle since its creation. The Holy Spirit we want to know is just like this. The Holy Spirit is God who is invisible but keeps our spiritual life, created the world of creation. Just as gravity is needed on this earth in which we live, the Holy Spirit is absolutely necessary for our spiritual lives. People understand the Holy Spirit non-personally. Some even have people who understand and interpret the presence of the Spirit as a force, a spirit that exists in nature. This is a great misunderstanding of the Holy Spirit. The Bible does not teach it that way. The Holy Spirit is not an impersonal being, but a personal being. The Holy Spirit has a personality. Because He is God.

On the personal side, the Holy Spirit is the one who knows everything (1 Cor. 2:10, 11). He is intelligent and mastered and knows all things. Second, the Holy Spirit has feelings (Eph. 4:30).

The Holy Spirit is grieved, rejoicing, grieving and judging, teaching, leading the chosen people, managing the world. Third, the Holy Spirit has a will. He is doing what is meant, and doing all things directly (1 Corinthians 12:11). Because the Holy Spirit is a personal being and God, everything is revealed when you stand in front of the Holy Spirit. He insights the depths of my soul, and knows me better than anyone else. He points out my transgressions and opens up the path to go when the Holy Spirit is with me on my wandering path.

LET US KNOW WHAT THE HOLY SPIRIT DOES AS A PERSONAL BEING.
(Romans 8:26; Acts 3:39; John 14:26; John 16:13)

The Holy Spirit who has a personal aspect always teaches us (1 Cor. 2:13). It is the one who tells us what we should do and what not to do. The Holy Spirit who teaches us is the first piece of evidence to prove to be a personal being. Second, the Holy Spirit himself petitions for us. It is the Prayer (Romans 8:26) for us. When we are weak and often fall down. When we do, we do not know what to do.

For us, the Holy Spirit himself asks the Father. And thirdly, miracles and signs still do (Acts 3:39). The Holy Spirit who works among us today shows us many miracles and signs, accepts Him as the Savior, and responds to our problems. The fourth is the one who helps us (John 14:26). Fifth, the ministry of the Holy Spirit personally helps and guides us (John 16:13). The Holy Spirit has been our shepherd so that we can help us to walk in the right truth and guide us to the right path.

WHAT IS THE NATURE OF THE HOLY SPIRIT TO PROVE TO BE GOD?
(Heb. 9:14; 1 Corinthians 2:10, 11; Psalm 139:7; Gen. 1:2; Luke 1:35; John 3:8; Romans 8:11)

The Holy Spirit is God. In the Bible, the work of the Holy Spirit comes from what God does. In the early church, the Holy Spirit worked for each man in the Pentecostal attic of the Mark. The Spirit of God has come to teach disciples. So now the Holy Spirit God comes to the hearts of disciples and does the work of God himself. Therefore, the Holy Spirit has God's character. He is eternal (Hebrews 9:14). He has been with us from the beginning and is eternal. And He knows everything (1 Corinthians 2:10, 11).

It is ubiquitous (Psalm 139:7). It is full of love, omnipotent, and merciful. He has the character of God and is among all believers. The Holy Spirit is working as God in equal place with God the Father and the Son Jesus Christ.

As the Trinity, the Holy Spirit supports the role of the Father God and the Son God and is subservient to one another. In the Chalcedon council in 451, and the Constantinople Council in 381, the Holy Spirit was God and at the same time declared to be equal to the Father God and the Son God.

The Holy Spirit is God Almighty. He who trusts in the Holy Spirit relies on God. It is important that we accept the Holy Spirit as a being. The Holy Spirit works in God. The person caught in this Holy Spirit recognizes God and enters into His power. We are standing in the midst of the Spirit. When we pray, the Spirit of comfort and grace flows to us. Through the Holy Spirit God is dwelling in the fullness of grace.

THE HOLY SPIRIT GOD MENTIONED IN THE WESTMENSTER CONFESSION OF FAITH.

First, the Holy Spirit comes from the Father and the Son of the Trinity of God, but has the same reality and is equal in power and glory. This Holy Spirit, together with the Father and the Son, believed, loved, obeyed, and worshiped for all ages. Second, he is the main, the grantor of life. It is everywhere and every good thought, pure hope. Third, God wants to give the Holy Spirit to anyone who wants to. This Holy Spirit is the only effect being in the application of redemption.

    He encourages men to regenerate with his grace, to confess their sins, to move their heart to confession, and to persuade and accept Jesus Christ by faith. He binds all believers to Christ and remains in them as a Comforter and sanctifier, giving them the Spirit of prayer. And doing all gracious works, whereby the saints are sanctified and sealed until the day of redemption.

[Meditation] The Power of the Holy Spirit

+ In the Old Testament and New Testament, what power did the Holy Spirit work with?
+ What important ministry is it still doing for us?
(Jn 16:8; Titus 3:5; 1 Corinthians 12:13; 1 Corinthians 6:19, 20; Ephesians 1:13, 14)
+ What ministry of the Holy Spirit does it as a helping hand? (Romans 8:16; Ephesians 1:17, 18; Romans 8:26, 27; 1 Corinthians 2:9, 10, 13; Ephesians 3:16-19; Romans 8:14)
+ Let's find out about the gifts of the Holy Spirit.
(1 Peter 4:10; Romans 12:6-8; 1 Corinthians 12:8-10; Ephesians 4: 11, 12; 1 Corinthians 12: 27-31)

CHAPTER 10

THE POWER OF THE HOLY SPIRIT
Psalm 62:5-8

IN THE OLD AND NEW TESTAMENTS, WHAT POWER DID THE HOLY SPIRIT WORK WITH?

The Spirit of Creation, the Spirit of Revelation

The Holy Spirit is an invisible God. He performs power as God. In the Old Testament, the Holy Spirit God helps creation.

As the spirit of creation, as in Genesis 1:2, he created the universe that helped God's creation. And in the spirit of revelation, he revealed the word of truth to the prophets.

In particular, King David said that the Spirit of God speaks through himself (2 Samuel 23:2). And the Spirit is the spirit of power. He poured out power to the people of God, and in the Old Testament, for a limited period of time; he was empowered to do the work of God (Joseph, Samson, Gideon, Daniel and so on).

In the New Testament, the Holy Spirit made Jesus Christ conceive in the body of the Virgin Mary. He also gave Jesus the power to do the work of God.

When Jesus was baptized, the Holy Spirit descended upon him (Luke 3:21, 22) and gave the power to accomplish the will of God. At Pentecost, the Holy Spirit in the Upper Room raised the winds and came to each man like a flame. Now the Apostles received the power of the Holy Spirit, and they spoke in tongues, prophesied, and performed many miracles and signs. The church was built. Those who have been filled with the Holy Spirit will receive the gospel to the ends of the earth. And the Bible we read says that Paul comes from the Spirit (Acts 28:25, Hebrews 3:7).

The first thing we need to do in doing God's work is to receive the fullness of the Holy Spirit.

WHAT IMPORTANT MINISTRY IS HE STILL DOING FOR US?

(Jn 16:8; Titus 3:5; 1 Corinthians 12:13; 1 Corinthians 6:19, 20; Ephesians 1:13, 14)

Jesus completed the work of redemption for the believers. He is incarnate, minister, die, resurrects, ascends, still praying for us and striving for the fulfillment of our salvation. Jesus ascended and sat on the Heavens, but the ministry of His salvation continues through the Holy Spirit. First, the Holy Spirit makes us realize our sins.

The Holy Spirit makes us aware of the seriousness of sin. And we desire righteousness and accept Jesus as our Savior. Second, the Holy Spirit makes us regenerate.

It connects the disconnected relationship with God and revives spiritual life again. Third, the Holy Spirit comes to be in us rightly (1 Corinthians 6:19, 20). It means coming to be with us. It is inherent in us, and it helps us live a new life and helps us. Fourth, the Holy Spirit baptizes us and makes us a body with Christ. Fifth, the Holy Spirit is our guarantee. We affirm that we are God's possession.

The ministry of the Holy Spirit: to know, to regenerate, to be together, to baptize, and to guarantee.

WHAT IS THE MINISTRY OF THE HOLY SPIRIT WHO HELPS US?
(Romans 8:16; Ephesians 1:17, 18; Romans 8:26, 27; 1 Corinthians 2:9, 10, 13; Ephesians 3:16-19; Romans 8:14)

The Holy Spirit is the 'paracletos': helper, advocate, prophet, lawyer who helps us. So the Holy Spirit is a "helper". Then what is the ministry of the Holy Spirit of the Comforter?

First, it helps us to be sure of our salvation (Romans 8:16). I am doubtful, but the Holy Spirit removes all these doubts and gives me confidence as a saved people. Second, when we read the Bible, he helps us to recognize and understand the Word. The Word is life. Reading the Word is to gain life. When the Word cannot be realized, so the Holy Spirit reminds us that we understand the Word and accept it.

Third, the Holy Spirit helps us to understand and accept God's will (Eph. 1:17). We want to know God's will in every way. We want to know what God's will is for us. At that time the Holy Spirit helped us to realize that this was the will of God. Fourth, the Holy Spirit helps us in our prayers. In Romans 8:26-27, when we do not know what to do with prayer, the Holy Spirit himself knows what our hearts desire on our behalf and instead asks God.

And the Holy Spirit leads us to pray for us so that we can pray according to the will of God (The prayer the Lord taught). Fifth, the

Holy Spirit helps us to obey the will of God and stand firm in our faith. The Holy Spirit helps us to come to God in order not to walk the wrong path of our children and not to disobey God. Sixth, the Holy Spirit awakens us in the way we do not know or can not imagine at all, we do it before, we support, and help us.

We humans are weak. We always encounter limitations. Every time we do that, the Holy Spirit has compassion on us and fulfills our needs in a way that we have never known. Therefore, we must live a life full of the Holy Spirit. What kind of life is the life filled with the Holy Spirit?

① in the Pentecostal Church, the filling of the Holy Spirit means the people who are touched by the Holy Spirit speak the tongues of each nation and fulfill the ministry of God through each gift.

② the saints must be filled with the Holy Spirit to live a victorious life. The way of the filling of the Holy Spirit of the saints is to dedicate their lives to the Lord entirely, to cut off all the sins in them and to completely eliminate them, to be eager to actively fill the Holy Spirit and to believe that we are filled with the Holy Spirit. It is accepting. Do not reject the Holy Spirit as your will.

③ the filling of the Holy Spirit is the word of Christ that should abound in us. Colossians 3:16 says, "Let the word of Christ dwell in your richly as you teach and admonish one another with all wisdom, and as you sing psalms, hymns and spiritual songs with gratitude in your hearts to God."

LET'S KNOW ABOUT THE GIFTS OF THE HOLY SPIRIT.
(1 Peter 4:10; Romans 12:6-8; 1 Corinthians 12:8-10; Ephesians 4:11, 12; 1 Corinthians 12:27-31)

The gift of the Holy Spirit is to fulfill its power so that the Saints are in need of more serving God, the Saints, and the Church. 1 Peter 4:10 says, "Each one should use whatever gift he has received to serve others, faithfully administering God's grace in its various forms."

God has given us the gift of the Holy Spirit to serve God, to serve the Church, for true fellowship with the saints, and for the testimony of the gospel. There are many gifts of the Holy Spirit. First, it is a gift of duty. This gift is an Apostle, Prophet, Evangelist, Pastor (Teacher) when it is interpreted according to the circumstances of the Early Church at that time. These are those who serve the church. In the service of the church, this gift lasts until the Lord comes.

Second, it is a gift of service. This is a non-transitory gift. In other words, it is a gift that does not require special miracle or target. These gifts should appear in the church many times. Gifts of service, gifts of counsel, teaching, relief, gifts of mercy, gifts of help, gifts of ruling etc.

Third, it is a special gift. It shows many miraculous aspects. It is supernatural, and sometimes this gift is also a present for those who are not receptive to the Gospel. For example, let Peter and John do many abilities, such as raising an impaired man sitting at the temple gate, healing, opening the door of the prison for evangelism, and allowing God to do the work. Healing, various abilities, prophecy, spiritual, dialect, interpreter etc.

Through the gift of the Holy Spirit, the fruit of the Holy Spirit is created. Love, joy, peace, patience, mercy, goodness, gentleness, temperance, loyalty, etc.

[Meditation] Trinity

+ Does the Bible say the Trinity?
+ What do you think of the Trinity?
+ Father, Son, Holy Spirit how can we explain God as a Trinity doctrine?
+ What does the Trinity doctrine mean for our faith?

PART II

CHAPTER 11

TRINITY
Exodus 20:1-6

DOES THE BIBLE MEAN THE TRINITY?

We can not think of God apart. God is one. But God exists in three persons. Three persons are not separated. God exists in three persons and in one essence.

However, if we meditate and study the Bible in detail, we can reach the conclusion that the Bible exists as a trinity about the existence of God.

The way God exists can be explained by Trinity doctrine. In the Old Testament, God is emphasized as one God. And only God is true of worship.

So in the Ten Commandments, from one commandment to four commandments speak of the commandment of God. "You shall not have other gods besides me (Exodus 20:3)." And when the Israelites were living in the wilderness, they heard the clear word of God through Moses.

It is said, "The Lord God is only one, that we should love Him with all our heart, with all our soul, and with all our strength (Deuteronomy 6:4-5)."

In 1 Corinthians 8:4, God is only one. In Ephesians 4:6, God is one, the Father of all, the unity of all, and all in all. Thus, the Bible clearly emphasizes that God is one. If we think of God's being as being divided, this will result in denial of both the Old Testament and the New Testament. The Bible certainly emphasizes that God is one.

WHAT DO YOU THINK OF THE TRINITY?

We know that God is one, both Old Testament and New Testament. There are things we can easily misunderstand. The first is to think of God as a person. In other words, because God is one, God becomes the Lord, the Spirit, and the Father. This is called 'modalism' in theological terms. Modalism is a theory that God, persons, has three roles at the same time. The modalist has already been condemned as heresy in the early church history. Trinity doctrine does not advocate modalism. What the Trinity claims is that God is one, but God's single way of being is compounded.

Second, this doctrine is also a doctrine condemned as heresy. That is, there are three gods. God is the subdivision. This is called 'tritheism.' This tritheism is a heretical assertion. People often have a misunderstanding of God's existence. There are those who have a modalist idea that God is one, and that He is also the Son and the Holy Spirit, but that God exists independently of God, the Son, and the Holy Spirit independently of the three Gods. Modalistic thinkers claim that Jesus suffered and died on the cross and that Heavenly Father suffered.

And the same conclusion comes to deny the whole Old Testament and the New Testament, claiming that those who claim tritheism are the only Heavenly Father.

FATHER, SON, HOLY SPIRIT, HOW CAN WE EXPLAIN GOD AS A TRINITY DOCTRINE?

The doctrine of the Trinity refers to the existence of three personal beings in one God. Each being is not separate, but each being in the presence of the other and become God at the same time. Most importantly, we share God's fuller nature. In the New Testament, Thomas refers to Jesus as God. He touched the side of Jesus and the wounds of his hand and confessed himself to be 'my Lord and my God.'

In addition, in the New Testament, Jesus told Himself as the Creator God, and Titus 2:13 referred to Jesus as 'our great God, Savior Jesus Christ.' The same is true of the Holy Spirit.

In Acts 5:3, 4 we speak of the Holy Spirit as being equal to God, especially to the Holy Spirit, to be holistic, omnipotent, and bearing the character of God. The great worker, Paul, also has a doctrine of the Trinity. Paul emphasizes that his ministry is a ministry of the Father, the Son, and the Holy Spirit (Matthew 28:19). What does this mean?

By connecting the Father, the Son, and the Holy Spirit, we explain the three persons by the equal person of God, and each person is connected by unifying them, not by being separated. God exists as one person and not as one person but as three persons.

As the first person in the doctrine of the Trinity, he leads the entire universe, and you are the master. In the ministry of creation and redemption, He is the one who plans and protects what is needed as the deliverer. The second role of the Father God is the ministry of the salvation of Jesus Christ. God, who is God, accomplishes salvation. God who comes as the Holy Spirit keeps the work of redemption constantly and protects the Saints. The role of the Father, the role of the Son, and the role of the Holy Spirit become one with each other and accomplish the plan of God the Father.

Westminster Ch 2, verse 3: God's body is one or three. One body, one power and one eternity. God as Father, God as Son, and God as Holy Spirit. The Father is not made up of, or comes out of, any substance. The Son is born from the Father forever, and the Holy Spirit comes from the Father and the Son for eternity.

WHAT DOES THE TRINITY DOCTRINE MEAN FOR OUR FAITH?

First, God is perfect and Almighty. We are explaining in the doctrine of the Trinity that God exists as a person and as three persons. This is the truth that shows that our God is perfect, absolute, powerful, and God who controls everything. We can not think of it as a bias.

Second, the Trinity means harmony. The God of the Father, the Son, and the Holy Spirit accomplishes the plan of God the Father through one ministry and at the same time the ministry of each person. The faith of the saints must also be one in harmony. We need to know that we can build Christian communities in a more beautiful way when we are in harmony among the Saints and as one body and one ministry.

[Meditation] Depravity and Salvation

+ Let us think about man as God's image (Genesis 1:27)
+ How did human beings fall, and were they polluted with sin? What does the Bible say about these people?
(Romans 5:12-25; 7:14-25)
+ Let us consider the fall of man and the meaning of the cross of Christ.
+ What is salvation?
+ Let's think about the way to salvation.

CHAPTER 12

DEPRAVITY AND SALVATION
Romans 5:12-21

LET US THINK ABOUT MAN AS GOD'S IMAGE (Genesis 1:27).

Someone caught the fish at night by the river. He wanted to eat meat very much. But there was a problem. There was no fire to cook the fish. He went to the neighbor's house in the middle of the night despite his reluctance to knock on the door.

The owner who was sleeping opened the door. In fact, he has caught the fish, but he wants to cook this fish, but he is here to borrow the fire. At the moment the owner laughed loudly said. You really are a fun person. Once you come to my house to borrow fire, look at what is in your hand. At the owner's hand, he saw his hand. There was a lamp in his hand to light the way at night.

The figure of the person who came to borrow the fire shown in this illustration can be seen as our appearance today. God left the image of God on our human being. But we humans are ignorant and foolish and do not believe in God. If we get close to God's Word, we know who we are. We will realize the truth. When God created the world, God was enough to make the world.

God created the world for the glory of God (Isaiah 43: 7). Therefore, our human purpose is to glorify God (Ps 16:11, 1 Corinthians 10:31). God is the spirit. The fact that human beings were created in the image of God is more evident in the following ways:

First, we have a ruthless discernment. It's clear about right and wrong. We have a conscience. Second, we are spiritual beings. God is the spirit. We have a physical body, but we can not live without the satisfaction of the Spirit. Therefore, humans always want to worship and want to serve. Third, we long for wisdom.

It is rational. We have a reasonable judgment. Animals do not think about the future. But humans prepare for the future.

Why? This is because we are rational and reasonable. Fourth, God is harmonized with the Trinity. The three persons are equal. And it exists together. Likewise, humans seek harmony. It is a social existence. Therefore, division or confrontation is an act that is out of harmony with the will of God.

HOW DID THE HUMAN BEING FALL, AND HAVE SINNED WITH SIN?

What does the Bible say about these people? (Romans 5:12-25; 7:14-25)

The human being in Eden is a man who does not fall down. They were created to live in harmony with God. It is Satan to break this harmony. Satan tempted Eve to face God. He has caused God to rebel. He has made a fool of God's command (command not to eat) and disobeys God's will. Because of this, man has come to the point where he can do evil, and the contaminated sin has led to all the descendants.

This is called 'total corruption.' This corruption is completely corrupted from the knowledge of God in all aspects, spiritual, intellectual, moral, and so on. The man without God has no hope. There is a lot of evidence that Godless man is completely corrupted. First, the absurdity of man without God is evidence of history. Many human civilizations came to the world, but most of them walked the road of rising and falling.

Second, our conscience itself shows us that we are sinners and that the nation is nothing. Third, we say that we can not do anything with our strength. No matter how people try to follow the values of the world. The pleasure of the flesh and the pleasure of enjoying it fully, but in the end, the nature of the fallen man do not enjoy a satisfying life. Fourth, the cross of Jesus Christ makes fools of people who do not repent. Saints who do not repent have no hope. There is no vision. Fifth, the Bible sees a man who sinned as having no hope.

"Everyone has sinned and can not reach the glory of God (Romans 3:23)."

LET US CONSIDER THE DEPRAVITY OF MAN AND THE MEANING OF THE CROSS OF CHRIST.

Without the fall of man, we can not think of the meaning of the cross of Christ. All human beings have lost their way to God by sin. It is the human being to wander without knowing the way. It does not know or believe God because of total corruption. No human being is saved. Christ is the God who came to restore the broken relationship between God and us. His ministry is the work of salvation. He cut off all the curses on the cross. The Lord has opened the way to God through the cross.

How much more, then, will the blood of Christ, who through the eternal Spirit offered himself unblemished to God, cleanse our consciences from acts that lead to death, so that we may serve the living God! (Hebrews 9:14; Ephesians 2:13; 1 Peter 1:18, 19; 2:24; Isaiah 53:5)

WHAT IS SALVATION?

People have wrong information about salvation. Some people claim that they can go to heaven even if they do evil. No matter what you do, everyone can go to the kingdom of God. This view is called universal salvation.

This view, however, is based on erroneous assumptions. The Bible makes it clear. According to Titus 3:5, "He saved us, not because of the righteous acts that we have done, but because of his mercy, according to the washing of rebirth and the renewal of the Holy Spirit."

This means that by human endeavor, it can not be saved. Revelation 20:15 says, "Whosoever is not written in the book of life is thrown into the lake of fire." Salvation is literally what I receive. It is salvation to rescue a person dying in water. There must be someone to rescue. It is Christ. Jesus Christ is the one who saved me from the death and saved me. We can not be saved unless Christ helps us.

LET'S THINK ABOUT THE WAY TO SALVATION.

The road to salvation is the way the saints should walk. It is God's blessing and guidance guaranteed to the Saints. The Saints have already been scheduled (predetermined) by God to be saved. God had a plan of salvation for us from the ages before he chose us and was saved. Therefore, this salvation we receive is based on God's through grace. Ephesians 2:8 "Because of this grace you have been saved through faith, not because of you, but because of God's gift." This salvation we have is the gift of God entirely.

This gift is from God. To enjoy this gift, you must trust the person who gave you the gift. If you do not know anyone and you receive a gift, you will start with suspicion first. But if you know who gave you the gift, you will rejoice, believe, and get the gift. It is the same. We trust Him when we know that He is the One who gave us the gift of salvation.

Trusting God means trusting in all of His, the Word, the works, and all of His power(Faith, 'pistis' entrustment, delegation). If we truly believe in God, we know that we are sinners before God. Because God is the Creator and the Creator of man. To believe in God is to meet someone who has made me. We know that the man God made is fallen and is in sin. Therefore, when we believe in and trust in God, we are bound to know that I am a sinner and confess my sins to Him. We receive Jesus, accept Him as the Savior, have faith and eventually lead to repentance, forgiveness, and salvation.

The saved Saints must now live in conviction. We must stand on clear conviction as a saved person. Those who are convinced know that God leads me and protects me like a pupil. This is to confess that God is the one who made us safe. Sometimes we get caught up in anxious worries.

Will I ever be forgiven by God? There are times of anxiety and fear that they will not be saved. Christians do not have to worry about this. Anyone who has committed a terrible sin that will not be forgiven will have nothing to do with his sin. In other words, it is insensitive to sin. But Christians take their sins seriously.

I think I have sinned. It is important to bear in mind that this mind has a longing spirit for sin forgiveness. Those who repent can receive forgiveness of sins. But disobedience, knowing that it is sin, but not deliberately repenting, eventually leads to judgment(God promises, plan of salvation, foundation of God's grace, faith in Christ, repentance, forgiveness, assurance, protection).

[Meditation] Change

+ What is change? Let's look for the dictionary meaning once.
+ How did I look before I believed in Jesus Christ? And how did I receive Jesus Christ as the Savior and changed me?
+ What privileges will the saved receive
(Ephesians 2:1, Romans 5:1, Ephesians 1:5)?

CHAPTER 13

CHANGE
1 Peter 4: 1-11

WHAT IS CHANGE? LET'S LOOK FOR THE DICTIONARY MEANING ONCE.

Water also rots in puddles if it does not move. It loses its vitality. Change is power. It is a powerful vitality that causes the dead to survive so that they do not die.

If there is a truth that does not change in this world, it is "there is nothing that does not change in the world". We have never been changed for a moment since the beginning of the year.

The lexical meaning of change is the change in shape, temperament, or condition. It can be said here that it includes everything that is alive. Just as everything is changing, we can not avoid change. A child becomes an adult and turns into an elderly person.

The same is true of nature. These changes do not give ultimate life. Everyone goes to the end. We will disappear. But the change caused by the Gospel is a change to live. We have to listen to the Gospel to get the life.

HOW DID WE LOOK BEFORE WE BELIEVED IN JESUS CHRSIT? AND HOW DID WE RECEIVE JESUS CHRIST AS THE SAVIOR AND CHANGED US?

A bar owner sold a store that had been running for a long time to a church organization. Church people took out the furniture that they used in the bar, put on a new light fixture, and put a chair in it. Soon after the repair was over, we were ready to do our first worship service.

But somehow, the parrot that the former owner grew up did not follow his master. This old and wise bird sits comfortably on the rafters and looks down at what is happening below.

When the worship began and the minister came in, the parrot mimicked the voice of a man and said, 'New master.' When the choir dressed in a gown came in, the parrot said 'a new actor, a new actor.' The parrot, who was looking down at the people sitting on the chair, said in a sad voice. "The same guests as before, the same guests as before (M. R. Dehan)."

We must have a clear difference after believing in Jesus Christ before we believe in Jesus Christ. Christ's change, regeneration is to die in the past sin and to be reborn as a new person. The new life is given, the identity is changed, and the person who lives for the mission God has given.

WHAT PRIVILEGE WILLS THE SAVED RECEIVE
(Ephesians 2:1; Romans 5:1; Ephesians 1:5)?

Those who are saved are those who are chosen by God.

God does not leave the chosen people. God is training. It changes the people whom God has chosen to serve, worship, and bear in the broad arms of God.

We, a sinner, cannot serve God. God hates sin. But he loves sinners. God hopes a sinful man to repent of sin and come before God. Those who are forgiven and humbled by him will no longer be ashamed of their sins, but they will be slaves of righteousness. They are trained not to lack in serving God. Just as God trained Moses in the wilderness to guide the people, and as Abraham was called out from the idolatry of Ur of the Chaldeans and trained as the ancestor of faith, God chooses and transforms his children today and uses them as God's workers. God is the one who transforms me. How does he change me?

First, as a people who have been saved by God, God gives us the privilege of making me as chosen people. In other words, he makes adoption of me. Being bilateral means being a member of a legitimate family. Even though the bloodline is not mixed at all, people adopt the child and raise the child with their own family register. Then the child becomes a legal child. Both inherit all rights of the parents. Likewise, we become the sons of God. We are basically born sinners.

It is a servant of sin. However, God has adopted me and is no longer a son of sin, but a child of God. I have nothing to pay. Jesus already paid for everything through the death of the cross. It is now being separated from Adam's family and becoming a family of God. As children of God, we enjoy all kinds of rights and privileges. We call God 'Abba' and 'Father (Rom 8:15).' In the Roman system, all the rights of the past are extinguished and the two inherit the rights of the new family, in other words, they are recognized as others who are completely different from the past.

Second, the changed ones are united in Jesus Christ. This is similar to the meaning that a woman marries and becomes one with her husband as Genesis 2:24 says. The same is true of our relationship with Jesus Christ. The word union with Christ says that I am crucified with Jesus, as in Galatians 2:20.

In Colossians 2:20 I am already believed to be dead on the cross with Christ, buried (Romans 6:4), raised again with Him (Ephesians 2:5), suffered with Him (Romans 8:17), received glory (Romans 8:17), and inherited rights as children of God (Romans 8:17).
As a child, he is also an heir, an heir of God, and an heir with Christ, and we must suffer with him to receive glory with him (Romans 8:17).

This means that they are not discriminated against. Those who are in Jesus Christ receive equal treatment from God. Third, God changes us and justifies us. God's justification for us is the grace of God. God's justification for us means forgiving our sins and calling us righteous by faith. Abraham believed in God. Because of this faith, God justifies Abraham.

Likewise, in Romans 5:1, we are righteous by faith, that is, through our Lord Jesus Christ, we enjoy peace with God. God builds Jesus as righteous. That righteousness will have an impact on all those who believe in Jesus Christ as Savior. I am a righteous man by faith in Jesus. Fourth, we receive the grace of new life and redemption. Life is again born. Jesus talked with Nicodemus. He has spoken of the secrets of regeneration. Rebirth is a Christian privilege. Regeneration is the spiritual rebirth of life. But there is an important element that must not be lost in regeneration. It comes from Ephesians 2:4-5. "God, who is rich in mercy, has raised us up with Christ, who died of transgression because of his great love for us, and you have been saved by grace." To be born again, I am not alone but I, it says. To live, Jesus Christ must be with me. I can not think of being born again without Christ. In order for my soul to live again, Jesus Christ must work for me, and his grace must come upon me. For those who have such a life, Jesus redeems us. The word redemption is 'seeking, belonging.'

If you want to know the exact meaning of this word first, it is 'agoraso.' This means buying from the market. It is Agorazo to buy things in the marketplace. No one goes to the marketplace without money.

You need money to buy things. It attaches the prefix 'ex' to this agora group. 'X' means outside. In other words, X-Agorazo means buying goods and coming out of the market. If you buy things and see things in the marketplace, you have to get out of there.

The following is an explanation of this once again. Our Lord Jesus Christ has gone to a marketplace where slaves are bound (the world of sin). Jesus found us trapped as slaves of sin. And to pay for ourselves, he paid for the value of himself (death of the cross).

And he comes out of the marketplace with us captive (Agora). And he frees us again. Freedom has given us a new eternal life and made us live again. This means that he has redeemed us and given us a new life.

[Meditation] The enemy we must fight against

+ What is Satan? (1 Peter 5:8; Isa 14:13-15)

+ What is demon being? (Isaiah 14:12-15; 1 Timothy 4:1-3)
+ What is the world like? (1 John 2)
+ Let's talk about the weakness of our bodies. Who came to bear the weakness?

CHAPTER 14

THE ENEMY WE SHOULD FIGHT AGAINST
Isaiah 14: 12-20

WHAT IS SATAN? (1 Peter 5:8; Isa 14:13-15)

Isaiah 14 speaks specifically about Satan's desires. Satan's desire is likened to the desire of King Babylon. The word 'Venus' is used to refer to the word 'a morning star.' The primary meaning is the king of Babylon. Sennacherib of Assyria had a desire to exalt himself and to shine brightly and to rule the world. This means Satan's desire. In Latin, the word 'morning star' is also used as the term 'luminous', or 'Lucifer.' Satan was a fallen angel caught in the desire and pride to become like God. These Satan also walk down the road from the text. The word 'fallen from heaven' refers to the triumph of Jesus Christ and the fall of Satan in spiritual terms.

Satan's ultimate desire can be said as follows. First, it is a symbol of pride. In 1 Timothy 3:6, Satan was an angel but rebelled against God. He wanted to be like God. It is the most evil being in the universe to be like God. God hates the pride.

Second, Satan always opposes God's will. He is also against all Christians who follow God. He is our enemy (1 Peter 5:8). Third, Satan has a strong ability. But that does not mean he is omnipotent. He is the one who caught authority. It is the spirit of disobedience (2 Corinthians 4:4). Fourth, Satan constantly interferes with the Saints so that believers do not hear the gospel and are not saved. The main goal is the believers. And he is ghosting to corrupt the Saints. Fifth, Satan is the spirit of deceit. They pretend to be an angel of light and ghosts to seduce the Saints and to fall away from the faith.

Jesus speaks of Satan as a liar, a murderer (John 8:44). Satan, therefore, will deceive the people and build their kingdom on earth (Ezekiel 28:13-19). Satan eventually kneels before Jesus Christ. And forever Satan will be judged.

Revelation 20:10 "And the devil which deceives them shall be thrown into the fire and the sulfur pail, and there shall be the beast and the false prophet, and shall be troubled day and night forever and ever."

WHAT KIND OF GHOST IS THERE?
(Isaiah 14:12-15; 1 Timothy 4:1-3)

Ghosts are evil spirits. Some theologians say that demons are angels who have fallen and sinned together when Satan is arrogant and rebels against God. Demons are a group of being who rebel against God's will and sympathize with Satan's will. There are some of these heretics who are deceiving us now, who are caught in the wrong ghosts. This is a misunderstanding about the identity of the ghost.

The demon makes people deceive as much as Satan spoke. It manifests itself in many ways as a spirit of deceit. That is why people misunderstand the reality of ghosts so they can not hear the gospel of Christ. In other words, the dead do not become ghosts, but evil spirits of Satan are pretending in many ways to delusive people. Satan is not omnipotent, but he has strong power.

He has a powerful army of demons (Mark 5:12; 1 John 3:8; Job 1:9-12). This army of demons travels all over the world and chooses those who will go to hell to prevent the way of faith. Some ghosts are attached to an individual to control all of the people, while some ghosts are totally opposed to God through the state.

There are countries like the Persians in the Bible and Babylon. Which can give illnesses but not all diseases can be interpreted only by the history of ghosts, because our bodies may become weakened and become sick, but one thing is that the illness has come to man.

It is not possible to avoid disease and death as a result of the sin of Eve's crime: to make a person demonized, to distinguish between psychosis and demon possession.

And to oppose God, to exert supernatural powers and to control the fate of those who obey him(Shaman, fortuneteller, Magic, Mystic, Religious, False Prophet etc(Matthew 9, 10, 17; Mark 6; Luke 8; Acts16; Romans1,)

The Bible says there are ghosts, Satan, and angels. And I do not talk about the existence of ghosts, the existence of Satan, the existence of angels. Clearly, the Bible speaks of their reality.

This is to tell us that we have an invisible spiritual world and that we must be against them. The important thing is that the Saints can overcome the forces of Satan and demons. Why? The Christ who is with me is greater than them. Ephesians 6:12 says this: "Our wrestling is not against blood and flesh, but against the rulers and authorities, the rulers of this dark world, and the spirits of evil in heaven."

Here the world is not the earth, the world we live in. The word world here is under Satan's control. Why is Satan's dominion a spiritual battlefield for us to fight? It is where Satan is ruled, and those who are under Satan's dominion do not believe in God because of the lust of the flesh, the lust of the eyes, the pride of life, as in 1 John 2, and walk in the path of the Fall. It is not related to the divine will of God. We interfere to know God's will in full.

The world that Satan dominates is always the opposite of the will of faithful Christians who follow God. It is an act of deception to God, commit all sins, and pursue the pleasures of the world. Those who obey God faithfully and serve him will naturally be separated from Satan's evil world.

LET'S TALK ABOUT THE WEAKNESS OF OUR BODIES. WHO CAME TO BEAR THE WEAKNESS?

There are those who misunderstand the Bible. There are those who think our flesh is evil and dirty. Our bodies are always against the will of God. But there is something important. Here our body is not our body. Just as the world does not mean the earth, our bodies do not mean our bodies.

Here, the word flesh is a willingness to deny God. And it is the power that leads to a sinful way. Those who live in the flesh are likely to become slaves of sin (Romans 7). And to rebel against the will of God. The fruit of death, the lust of the flesh, the desire in Galatians 5, the work of the flesh, fornication, filthiness, lust, idolatry, trickery, enemies, conflict, Separation, heresy, speculation, drunkenness, prodigality, and takes us to a place that is not God's law. We are weak. So we have no choice but to be dragged away when the body fools us. We must not lose spiritual tension in order not to be in the flesh.

We must always win by the power of Jesus Christ. The Lord Himself took care of our weaknesses. We have to fight our flesh with our own strength that our weakness is in charge of the Lord, but Jesus means that the Lord has provided us with enough strength to fight and defeat the flesh. In the spiritual battlefield of the world, we fight if we fight, but the Lord supports us, and now we are triumphant by the power of the Lord.

[Meditation] The Secret of Victory

+ What you need for a spiritual battle is a weapon to use in a battle with a trained army. If you want to become a military, you need to have basic strength. Who can get the basic strength through? (Eph 6:10)
+ In order to battle, you need to know exactly who you are. Let us think about the devil's trick (Ephesians 6:11, 12).
+ We need spiritual battle equipment. What is it? (Ephesians 6:13-17)
+ What is more necessary than spiritual battle equipment (Ephesians 6:18-20)?

CHAPTER 15

THE SECRET OF VICTORY
1 John 5:18-21

WHAT IS NEEDED FOR A SPIRITUAL BATTLE IS A WEAPON TO BE USED WITH A TRAINED ARMY.

If you want to become a military, you need to have basic strength. Who can get the basic strength through? (Eph 6:10) Man has two serious misconceptions about Satan.

The first is that man is making Satan an object of fear that he is too big not to be able to win, and secondly, he is misunderstanding Satan as being too light and nothing. The Saints are children of God who receive Jesus Christ as their Savior and are saved. From the moment the Saints become children of God, we will go to a great spiritual battlefield. There we fight spiritual warfare against evil Satan. This is an inevitable battle.

If we are not children of God, children of righteousness, but still slaves of sin, and live according to the world and the flesh, we do not need spiritual warfare. For the servant of sin means that he belongs to Satan, and he can not be saved even if it is but he goes into eternal judgment with Satan.

But we were saved from hell punishment. We belonged to the world, and now we are a child of righteousness. Our identity has changed. Satan constantly blames us. So the saved Saints cannot avoid the spiritual warfare against Satan's evil entities.

Soldiers are harshly trained before they go to battle. As a soldier, he learns basic tactics and has discipline so that he will not be attacked by enemies in battle. And if you are a soldier, you will get a basic strength to get a strong physical condition. The Saints are similar. Christians must be prepared for basic physical strength before spiritual battle. After getting a basic strength, you will be trained as a necessary soldier on it. The Bible tells the basic strength needed by Christians in a spiritual battle:

"You are strengthened in the Lord and in the power of his strength (Eph 6:10)."

This means that Christians in the Lord are strengthened. The power of that it is the power through Jesus Christ.

We can not be strong on our own. But Christians are strengthened through the power of Jesus' cross and the power of the triumph of resurrection. To win in spiritual battle, the Saints must know the grace of salvation through Jesus Christ and stand on the cross and the faith of the Resurrection. This faith is the foundation of the Saints to win in spiritual battle. The devil is most afraid of the cross and the resurrection.

In order to win, we must first be caught up in the great grace of Jesus Christ. We need to know the grace of Jesus. The power of the gospel must be in me.

LET US THINK ABOUT THE DEVIL'S TRICK

In order to be in battle, you need to know exactly who you are. Let us think about the devil's trick(Ephesians 6: 11, 12).

The trick of the devil (Satan) means an evil plot. The devil is a liar. He is the deceiver of the saints. It is against the truth that it opposes God. So, if we are caught in the hands of a devil, we will be deceived by the devil forever and eventually abandoned by the devil. The devil does not observe all means and methods to overthrow the faith of the saints. And to win, we will do our best.

He will mobilize the rulers and powers of this world, the rulers of the dark world, and the evil spirits in heaven. The mobilization of rulers, powers, rulers of darkness, and evil spirits in heaven means that the forces of Satan are powerful.

The trick of the devil: 2Timothy 2:26; Romans 6:14; Romans 7:14; Gal. 5:19-21; Psalm 1:6.

The activity of the devil: Job 9:23; Job 1:5-10; Matthew 4:24; Matthew 8:28, 29; Ephesians 6:10, 11; 2 Thessalonians 2:11-12.

SPIRITUAL BATTLE EQUIPMENT IS REQUIRED. WHAT IS IT? (Ephesians 6:13-17)

Armor is required to go to war. Armor protects you from enemy weapons. In the text, you are asked to wear a full armor to win the spiritual battle. The whole armor protects the whole body. If there is a small gap, it attacks mainly there. We also have fragile parts.

Some people have weak points to be attacked. These parts are the main attack targets of Satan. Therefore, in order not to give an opportunity to Satan, you must wear a full armor.

First, we need a string of truth. It is wrapped around the strained waist here. It is necessary equipment to insert the sheath. And the belt is a necessary thing to use force. We must always prepare the Word of the Bible truth. Power comes from the truth. The power to defeat the enemy is in Scripture truth.

"Exhort the waist of your heart and obey it fully to the grace to be brought to you when Jesus Christ appears(1 Peter 1:13)."

Second, we must have a breastplate of righteousness. A breastplate is a tool to protect your heart. The chest is very important as part of the body. It is a place directly connected with life. God has granted us righteousness through Jesus Christ. It is the righteousness of Jesus Christ that guarantees our life that we attach the breastplate of righteousness.

Protecting from sin, protecting spiritual life, protecting from the attack of Satan, God assures us through righteousness.

Third, we need shoes in peace. Roman soldiers marched for a long time. So their mind and body were always tired. Good shoes are needed when marching. Without good shoes, they could not walk for a long time.

Good shoes of peace means that Jesus' peace will protect us everywhere we go. "I bring peace to you, my peace I give unto you. It is not as the world gives that I give it to you. Do not be troubled or terrified in your heart(John 14:27)."

Fourth, we need a shield of faith. Roman soldiers used circular shields. The shield protects the whole body. It protects from knives and various weapons safely. The evil Satan constantly attacks us in spiritual battles. Faith is needed to stop this. We must use faith as a shield to prevent Satan's attacks. Fifth, you must use the helmet of salvation. There is an important part of the body, which is the head part. It is the most vulnerable place. If your head hurts, it can have catastrophic consequences.

In our faith, when the clear conviction of salvation is shaken, there is a crisis in our spiritual life. We must be sure that God has already given us salvation and life. We must be sure that he has forgiven us from past sins and has freed us from punishment.

We must be sure to free us from our present sins, and we must not doubt that he will free us from future sins. Sixth, there must be a sword of the Spirit. Roman soldiers mainly used double-edged swords. It also cut and stung. It is the main weapon to attack the opponent in the battle. It is the only weapon that can attack. Bands, breastplates, shoes, shields, and helmets are usually required for defense but are required for various attacks. Sometimes we have to fight against the devil. It is not a thing to avoid.

The Holy Spirit is against the devil. A person who is overwhelmed by the power of the Holy Spirit can defeat the devil. Battle requires defensive weapons and attacking weapons. It is also necessary for spiritual warfare. Please check the status of your spiritual weapons at once. What is the weapon I lack?

WHAT ARE THE MOST NECESSARY THINGS BESIDES SPIRITUAL BATTLE EQUIPMENT (Ephesians 6:18-20)?

First, prayer! The apostle Paul says: "Make all prayers and supplications, always praying in the Holy Spirit, seeking for it, and always seeking for the saints." In order to win in spiritual battle, prayer is needed. Prayer is not limited. We must do 'every prayer and supplication.' This means that we must actively seek out the Lord.

There are a lot of strategies and tactics to win. There are many ways to do this. Only for victory alone. As such, prayer has an active aspect. We must pray in the Spirit. Ignore means that you are not always on time. 'Watch and seek.' This is prayer zeal. Pray for the saints. This is not a prayer for yourself but a prayer for your partner. In war, we do not fight alone. There are spiritual co-workers. We must pray for their victory. Second, to know the secrets of the gospel. Those who know the secrets of the gospel are those who know God's will clearly. Third, it is a clear call. Paul calls himself bonds to the gospel. He was convinced by the clear call.

[Meditation] Take off the spiritual snare!

+ In Lesson 5, we looked at the reality of the enemies we should fight and the equipment needed in spiritual battle. In spiritual training, the process of being polished as a military comes.
+ Let's think about the meaning of the military. An army is a place that has been reborn as a soldier away from the world. It is a place to receive training. There is a process that must go through to get trained as a soldier.
+ What is the spiritual snare we should take off?
(Things that interfere with the life of faith)

CHAPTER 16

TAKE OFF THE SPIRITUAL SNARE!
Mark 1:16-20

In Lesson 5, we looked at the reality of the enemies we should fight and the equipment needed for spiritual battle. In spiritual training, the process of being trained as an army comes.

SOLDIERS OF CHRIST

In worship, preaching, prayer, and praise, we hear the bride of Christ as an idiom.

We may be dreaming of being a pure bride who will someday be prepared to meet the bridegroom. But we must also remember that the Lord called us to be the soldiers of Christ. Especially, it is not easy or natural for men to meditate on being a bride. What does it mean to be a soldier? Soldiers are people who fight and fight in a war to defend the nation and the people. It would be the same to be a soldier of Christ. We must protect the kingdom of God from the forces of evil spirits and safeguard its people. If our struggle is not about blood and flesh, but about the differences between heresies, wrong authority, the rulers of this dark world, and the spirits of evil in heaven, our enemy is only an invisible spiritual being, a spiritual influence.

If you do not fight, you have to retreat. If you can not keep it, you will lose it. If you can not win, you lose. There is no middle in the war.

Just as a soldier is always on his guard against the enemy, we must be alert. Always be prepared to check every corner of your life and to be able to run to the Lord's call at any time. Only then can we preserve the kingdom of God and protect ourselves and our churches.

LET'S THINK ABOUT THE MEANING OF THE ARMY.

An army is a place that has been reborn as a soldier away from the world. It is a place to receive training.

There is a process that must go through to get trained as a soldier. If there are no soldiers in the country, there will always be a national crisis in that country. Therefore, there must be a soldier who defends the country. It is the oldest system in human history. It is guarded by a highly trained soldier. Soldiers are not just born. It is trained. We invest a lot of money to make one soldier in the country.

It is said that more than one billion dollars are invested to make air force pilots in our country. Creating such a well-trained soldier is a costly, material and time-consuming price.

We enter the training camp to become a soldier. When you enter the training camp, all the things you have used in the world are collected. We take off all our clothes, things, cell phones, and even underwear, and only receive items that are paid by the military. What does this mean? It is to distinguish. Is to be isolated from the world. To be a spiritual military, we must live a life that is thoroughly separated from the world.

Now we are not the only one who has stayed in the past sin. We are a soldier who entered the training camp to be trained as a good soldier of Christ Jesus. We still use the things we used in the world. It does not break the sinful nature of sin. Then it is difficult to train as a good soldier.

WHAT SPIRITUAL SNARE DO WE NEED TO TAKE OFF?
(Things that interfere with the life of faith)

In ancient times, there was a time when rodent was placed to catch a mouse. Ordinary rat poison is put in the tasty meat. However, dogs often eat rodenticide and die. So, when a master tried to train a dog, he put the meat in front of the dog and tried to eat it.

Repeating these dozens of times, dogs do not eat meat anymore. If he put a meat in front of a dog, now a dog is looking at the owner's face and will not eat. In the end, the untrained dogs in the village died of rodent poisoning, but the trained dog didn't die.

There are times when God also gives us drudgery. If God is good, he would be willing to do this for us. But it is a blessing exercise to have us. Because looking at God is the essence of faith, and that is the only way we do not perish.

For a dog, meat is a good food. Meat tempts the dog visually, olfactory, and tastefully. An untrained dog will eat the meat if it is on the meat, and will die. However, trained dogs do not. Because it has been trained, self-controlled. It is visible but controls itself so it does not get in eyes. It is good to eat, but the smell stimulates one's desire, but it has been thoroughly exercised because it has been trained. Satan walks with so many nooses to seduce the saints. He gathers all the things that can give all the pleasures of the world and he seduces the Saints with the prize. On top of that, there are things to kill souls. Those who are not trained as soldiers of Christ are led by their own greed to eat the food of the deadly poison that Satan has prepared, but the trained Christians can boldly defeat the temptation of Satan no matter how tempting. There are snares that bind us.

First, it is the lasso of intelligence. We always have doubts about the Word of God. I do not understand it with my knowledge. How can the world be created in one word, how the creatures enter into the ark, the water splits, and the dead are raised. By his own experience, knowledge cannot understand the Bible and it is impossible. The Bible is not read by knowledge, but by faith. Second, our obsession with matter can become a lasso. A person needs a substance to live, but not a slave of matter. Satan knows very well that man is weak to matter. So he tests human beings with these weapons. Third, our spiritual despair, discouragement becomes a lasso. When prayer is not answering, when there is no progress of faith, when difficulty comes, we are trapped in a trap.

Spiritual discouragement drives me into a tremendous despair. There is a way to overcome this. First, we must acknowledge our own limitations. We know that we are a fragile person and we need to know that we can not overcome ourselves.

It is considered contradictory to recognize that I am weak and to have a military attitude. There is a man who thinks how a soldier can have a fragile appearance. To acknowledge my weakness does not mean I am not a strong soldier. To acknowledge my weakness is to acknowledge that only God is the one who will win this war. It must be a good tactician to win a soldier in a war. There must be a strategist. You must have a commander. God is such a being.

I can not, but I rely on God, my tactician, strategist, commander. A strong soldier is well-obedient and faithful to command. Next, we need a perspective that is seen from the perspective of God. God wants us to win. Therefore, we must believe that the God who gives victory is in me. The moment we are confident that we are on the side of God; Satan is already supposed to be in the war. Finally, it is to recognize that hardship is important. A difficulty is important to us. When we are in trouble, there are two eyes that pay attention to us. One is the gaze of demons.

What happens is they are watching. They want us to fall into trouble and stand on their side. Another eye is the eye of God. When we overcome difficulties and all the advanced who have won by faith will rejoice and are glad to see our victory.

"Therefore, there are many witnesses that surround us like clouds, taking away all the heavy and the sins that are easy to be entangled in, and racing before us with patience(Hebrews 12: 1)."

[Meditation]

Beloved believers! I want you to understand the entire lasso around you. The temptation of sin can be your lasso. The grace of spiritual depression in dealing with the life of faith is depleted, and a lasso becomes spiritually exhausted. If I feel a lasso around my beliefs, I want to lay down everything and have time for personal recovery with

God. God will help us. After this time, we will have faith like a warrior of faith like David, like pure gold, like the work of Job.

CHAPTER 17

METHODS OF SPIRITUAL TRAINING
Hebrews 10:32-36

Christian Existentialist philosopher Kierkegaard: There are two kinds of Christians. One is to imitate the life of Jesus Christ, to diligently resemble him, and the other is simply that there are cheap Christians who admire the life of Jesus and are satisfied with it.

We must do our best to our spiritual growth. Spiritual growth is to be accomplished by all the saints. Spiritual growth means life imitating Christ.

As we grow, we become Christ like. Our life is filled with the scent of Christ. Therefore, in order to grow, we must do our best. The 16th lecture looks at various ways in our spiritual training.

WHY SHOULD WE BE IN TRAING?

Training makes people tough. Soldiers must be well trained in military training. Athletes need regular training to get good grades and levels in the game. Students studying are enthusiastic about their studies and are required to achieve their skills.

All of this is because training is free in any fields. If a soldier is not trained, if an athlete is not trained, he or she will fail to their accomplishment. I feel insecure and nervous about being unable to train on the battlefield, at the stadium, and at school. So to be free from these things you have to build up your training well. If we build up spiritual training of faith, we are free from the temptation of the devil. It is free in the truth. It is also free from relationships with people. A person who has not been trained in spirit is put to the test, and it strengthens others as well as him.

KEEP THINGS AWAY FROM OUR SURROUNDINGS.

You need to keep things away from your surroundings that interfere with your spiritual life.

There are things that interfere with the spiritual life of modern Christians. First, for spiritual growth, it is important to create an environment in which I can grow spiritually.

TV, movies, computers, cell phones, music, and so on. Some people use the mass media to listen to God's words and listen to praise. There are those who think. Of course, the mass media may help us in our faith. Through the mass media, we can hear God's Word and listen to praise. But if the illumination of our inner life is not done first, the mass media will be only a temporary solution. There are those who try to fill our empty hearts with the media without growth without the illumination of inner life.

Henry David Thoreau, a famous poet of the 19th century, points out that today people are trying to fill their inner lives from external things(world concerns, mass media heard in the world). This means that reflection from deep inside must be done first for his inner growth. Spiritual discipline is to me how I find the voice of God, the will, and how close to God. Spiritual growth that resembles the Lord is internal. It is my inner side to resemble. Personality. I must be filled with the character of the Lord within me.

You should not use your favorite mass media as a primary textbook for your spiritual growth.

SPIRITUAL TRAING CAN BE DONE THROUGH MEDITATION.

Meditation is to meditate deeply on the Word of God. We must discover the truths contained in God's Word, the Bible. It is not simply reading. We must go down deep into the fountain of the Word.

Why did God ask the Israelites to come close to the Book of the Law (Deuteronomy 6:1-9) because the Word is life? It is a form of spirit. Meditate and meditate on the Word and apply it to my life. It is most necessary for spiritual growth.

SPIRITUAL TRAINING CAN BE DONE THROUGH PRAYER.

Why should we pray? A prayer is a holy act that affects me and God. Prayer is supplication. If I do not ask the Father, I and the Father have nothing to do. If the child does not ask for the parent, the child will no longer receive anything from the parent. Prayer is talking to God. It is asking and seeking for God's will. The word praying is also found in the Bible (Matthew 6:5-15). Prayer is what God most desires (Luke 18:1-8).

God loves those who pray. God sometimes makes us pray to train us. He deliberately brings me to trouble and knees before God. Those who are zealous in prayer, those who are loyal to prayer are well-trained.

FASTING

Fasting is sometimes necessary for spiritual training.

The Bible tells us about fasting: "Is not this the kind of fasting I have chosen: to loose the chains of injustice and untie the cords of the yoke, to set the oppressed free and break every yoke (Isaiah 58:6, 7)?" Fasting makes me sincere in front of God. Appetite is the most basic human desire. If we suppress appetite, we can naturally suppress other needs, says the Dutch theologian Thomas A Kempis. There is a covet of eating. However, we must abstain from this and go to the holy desire for God. God said that true fasting controlled our desire through the Word and extended it to the relationship between God and us. Soldiers are not free to ration food on the battlefield. Athletes also control their food, which is a discipline to deny oneself.

SIMPLIFYING

We need to simplify ourselves from the worldly things. What does simplicity mean? We do not think of many things. It is only one thing to pursue. Simplicity sometimes means humility. It means a restrained life that is not over-dressed and does not show off.

It is very helpful in spiritual training. But there are people who misunderstand this simplicity.

We consider simplicity to be too ambitious. We choose the penance of the flesh, completely disconnected from the worldly ones. This is rather a simplification of complexity. Simplicity is to give self to Christ. It is emptying oneself. It means emptying oneself, but being filled with Jesus Christ in the emptiness.

The child listens to the parents and starts organizing the room. This is a problem from now on. I do not know where to start. What do you do then? First of all, we start throwing away. Throw away what is useless and shrink. This is the principle of simplicity. Things that are misplaced in me, things that interfere with spiritual training should be thrown away. It needs to be unified. Then we accept the truth.

Those who are accustomed to simplicity now regain a one-to-one relationship with God. Everything around me was removed. I have abandoned things that interfere with fellowship with God. Now we must restore the one-on-one relationship with God. I am standing in front of God alone. Sometimes silence is needed to restore the one-on-one relationship with God. We must be quietly training to listen to the voice of God alone speaking inside.

God gives me the equipment I need. It is kind of listening aid equipment. It blocks all other sounds of the world and only perceives the sound heard from God. It is important for us to have time alone for spiritual training. It does not matter what time it is. It is a deep spiritual fellowship with God at the time when you are not the most obstacles to calling the name of God.

OBEYING

We must obey. In spiritual training, it is as important as obedience.
 Obedience should know who to obey. Obedience is based on truth. Is it true that I truly deserve to be obeyed? So obedience is my voluntary act. If you do not obey, you will be subject to the selfish self. Those who are not obedient insist on their own. This is not the correct attitude of obedience.

REPENTING

We must repent. In spiritual training, repentance means a new beginning. Repentance is a holy act that finds true self before God. If you repent, you will recover.
 He must be seen as qualified to receive spiritual training when he acknowledges his mistakes in spiritual training and seeks forgiveness before God.

WORSHIPING

You can do spiritual training through worship. We can say that worship is restored if it is a place where we gather and pray in the name of Christ, and where spiritual fellowship takes place, such as daily worship, regular worship, and Sunday worship and so on. Through the Word of Worship, we meet with God. And I want to live God-centered life.

A GOOD ATTITUDE

In order to do good spiritual training to God, we need a good attitude. It is because the blessing of God can be blessed. It means to recognize God as the master of life and to live. It is important for us to live in the real life, but it is important for us to live in spiritual training because it is our testimony that I am the child of God by giving to the Lord what we need most.

[Meditation] Definition of the Church

+ What do you think about the church?
+ Does the Bible define the Church in several ways?
(Romans 12:4, 5; Ephesians 2:19-22; Revelation 19:6-9)
+ What is the mission of the church?
(2 Tim. 3:16, 17; Acts 2:42; Acts 22:16; 1 Corinthians 11:23-26; 1 Corinthians 5:1-13)

CHAPTER 18

DEFINITION OF THE CHURCH
Ephesians 2:19-22

WHAT DO YOU THINK ABOUT THE CHURCH?

St. Augustine said, The person who does not consider the church to be a parent is a man who does not serve God without a father. For Christians, the church has a very important meaning. In other words, without the church, there is no spiritual basis for our faith. It is the foundation of faith. People go to the nearest market to buy what they need. They buy goods there. But the product does not come from anywhere.

The raw materials of the goods enter the factory and come out from there. The original place where the product was made is the factory that is produced immediately.

The food we eat is also where we are originally made. Faith is the same. There is a place where faith is gained and faith grows. God has appointed the place as a church on this earth. We have faith in the Church through Jesus Christ, and we grow into the precious fruit of God. Therefore, those who are good at church life are mature in their faith and know the secrets of faith well.

Some people are misunderstood about the church. We say that we attend church. Which church do you go to? But we have to answer this, and it becomes a more accurate answer. I am living a faith in the church. Here, the life of faith is everything. Being like Jesus, as a member of the Church community, means all the collective life that helps or serves other people's faith. The church is like a spiritual factory. The church is making me. The church builds my faith and dwells in the truth through there.

We are refining faith, personality, and life through the church. The head of the church is Jesus Christ. The owner of the church is Jesus Christ. In other words, Jesus Christ, the head of the church, makes the faith matures to grow. We are going to the church in order to be transformed through my faith and grow up as an example of Christ. We have nothing to do with us when we step on the church yard diligently. As we come out of the church, as the years of faith are piled up, more of the character of Christ should be buried in me. In this sense, the church has an important meaning.

DOES THE BIBLE DEFINE THE CHURCH IN SEVERAL WAYS?
(Romans 12:4, 5; Ephesians 2:19-22; Revelation 19:6-9)

When we came to the Old Testament and the New Testament, we learned the outward appearance of the church. The original appearance of the church is the basis of the church. They built a stone altar and called the name of the LORD there. Noah, Abraham, Enoch, and so on, many advanced believers built an altar and prayed to God.

Next, through this period of tribulation, we go to the time of the Tent for Meeting. It is the tabernacle. In the wilderness of Israel, there was always a tabernacle in the center of the people's journey.

These days of Tabernacle will be fixed to one place later. Solomon built the temple. This temple is fixed in one place and serves as a place to worship God. This temple age has been established in our hearts since Jesus came. Jesus built the temple of God in our hearts. Therefore, the holy place in me is the conversion of the Holy Spirit(Tent, Tabernacle, Temple, Holy Spirit).

First, the church can be compared to architecture (Eph. 2:19-22). There are many churches in the world. There are many churches over 1000 years in Europe. The church building has not collapsed until now.

And under the church, there are buried the servants of the Church who have been serving the church. The name is engraved on the stones. Church architecture is a symbol. Some say that the home is also a church. That's right. It says that the place where two or three people are gathered is also one church. This is also true. It is a church that two or three people gather together in the name of Jesus Christ to worship together. In addition to this, in Ephesians 2 of the Bible, as a full-fledged church, Jesus is the cornerstone, and the building in which the building is connected is called the church in full sense.

Second, the church is one body (Romans 12:4, 5). The body means having a sense of body. The place where two or three people gathered was also called the church. Then, two or three people can be separated. They are joined together in Christ to form a body.

We must work in harmony when doing God's work. Everyone belongs to Christ. One person is important because it belongs to Christ. It is the church that is loyal to ministries of various gifts for the glory of the Lord. Third, the church is the bride (Revelation 19:6-9). The church is 'ecclesia.' The word 'ek' is from the outside. 'Caleo' is a call. This is called from. It is the place where people gathered in the name of Christ. It is a gathering place distinguished from the sin of the world. Look at the bride. The bride has to keep her sanctification before marriage. From the moment of being appointed as a bride, it is preparing as a man's wife. It is called to distinguish it as the wife of a man. The church in this land is the bride of Christ. It is a holy place. To meet the bridegroom, Jesus Christ, all the saints in the Church live as brides. It is living apart from the world.

Fourth, the church should be a universal, local church. In the Bible, the meaning of the church is further extended to the saints themselves in the sense of the building of the people. Everyone who is a universal church worships those who confess Jesus Christ as a Savior and becomes a member of the Church. There is no discrimination and the threshold is not high.

Only those who confess Jesus as Savior are places where they come to know and gain eternal life without distinction. To be local is to be a church serving the area. Jesus also ministered to public ministry and went to the local church to teach the Word. Therefore, the term 'local' means a church serving the area, a church that regularly meets together to worship, and church service to help the souls in spiritual life.

WHAT IS THE MISSION OF THE CHURCH?
(2 Tim. 3:16, 17; Acts 2:42; Acts 22:16; 1 Corinthians 11:23-26; 1 Corinthians 5:1-13)

First, the church must teach diligently (2 Timothy 3:16, 17). It is the church that teaches the word of truth diligently.

Second, the fellowship of the saints should be well done in the church. It must be a union. A beautiful fellowship of faith must be made among the Saints (Acts 2:42).

Third, the church is a place of worship. It is a place to worship God. Under the name of Jesus Christ is a place where saints gather to worship God and confirm that they are children of God.

Fourth, the church is a place to serve (Galatians 6:10). "Therefore, as we have the opportunity, do good things to all, but to more families of faith." The Early Church was seen serving each other.

When they showed each other, they became a big example of the region and unbelieving people gathered fruit from the church. Therefore, when the unbelieving people come to the church, they must be served in such a way that they feel burdened. Believers should serve each other in such a way that if they come to the church, they will have a holy burden because of those who serve them and that they should do the same. Fifth, the church is the place where the Holy Communion is given. It is Jesus who has allowed the Lord's Supper.

Sixth, the church is baptized. The church of Christ is doing the Lord's Supper and Baptism in the name of Jesus.

Seventh, the church is a place for discipline and exhortation. If there is a saint who commits wrong sins, the Church must correct the sins of the saints. The church is the place where parents act. God has made us parents and heals the wrongs, but God does sometimes raise our children strictly through the church.

So the church is called to be disciplined saints. A saint who commits a wrongful sin should make a discipline at the governing body of the church so that the saints may repent and receive the comfort and grace of a greater God, and spiritually instruct them not to go astray. Discipline is done for the whole ministry. Sometimes we discipline ourselves personally, we do it publicly in the governing body (the session). Today, the modern church has lost its discipline. This is a real concern. The Early Church prevented the spiritual fall of the Saints through discipline, which enabled the church to grow healthier.

[Meditation] Sacraments and Church Workers

+ Why is baptism given (Acts 22:16; Titus 3:5)?
+ What does it teach in the Lord's Supper? (1 Corinthians 11:23-26) Let's think about the Lord's Supper's view.
+ Who is the church leader?
+ What conditions should leaders have? (1 Timothy 3:1-7; Titus 1:5-9)

CHAPTER 19

SACRAMENTS AND CHURCH WORKERS
1 Timothy 3:1-7

The sacrament is the manifestation of the covenant of grace, which God has ordinarily instituted in order to manifest Christ and His grace and to confirm his help in it.

At the same time it is a visible sign given to distinguish between those who belong to the Church and those who belong to the world.

It was also enacted to enable the Saints to serve God in Christ according to the word of God(Westminster Chapter 27 Section).

The Church is a community of God's children who have confessed Jesus Christ as Lord of faith and have been saved.

It is a place of common interest and one purpose. Its purpose is not to differ, but to glorify God, and to do the work of God. To this end, we are called. Because the church is holy, one can serve this church. It is only where the Saints who believe in Christ serve. To prove that you are a Christian, you must first be circumcised. It means the seal of the Holy Spirit. The baptism of the Holy Spirit is given from above to those who confess Christ.

There is another saying that we are Christians in public places (churches). 'Baptism' is a sacred act like a confession of faith. It is a confessional act in front of all men that I will be reborn as a Christian from now on. By being baptized, we become members of the church in Christ's church.

Those who are baptized will participate in the Lord's holy supper. By participating in the Lord's Supper, we are once again able to identify ourselves as Christians who have been saved. Baptism and the sacrament are so important.

WHY IS BAPTISEM GIVEN (Acts 22:16; Titus 3: 5)?

In the second century, in the document 'The Teachings of the Twelve Apostles (Tadake),' if you can not immerse yourself in water, you should baptize three times with water in your head only in the name of Father, Son, and Holy Spirit. It is said that you can do it instead. And in the days of the early church that persecuted Christians, it was not easy to celebrate baptism. Baptism is of equal importance.

Everything is meaningful. The important thing is the baptism that takes place inside. It is the baptism of the Holy Spirit.

Outward baptism is publicly recognized in the presence of the saints. It is important to believe in Jesus Christ and receive salvation inwardly rather than biased toward formal(Strength on the cross). Baptism is a sign that sin has been cleansed internally.

"Now what will you do? Get up and be baptized in the name of the Lord and cleanse all your sins (Acts 22:16). And being baptized indicates that you have received life spiritually from the Lord (Titus 3:5). He has cleansed our sins. He brought us into salvation by living the Holy Spirit in us and giving us new joy. It is not because we deserve to be saved.

God has graciously and mercifully saved me. Baptism tells us that I am one with Christ. Christ has risen again in me. Through Him, have been forgiven of sins, have eternal life, desire for resurrection, and have become citizens of heaven.

WHAT DOES THE LORD'S SUPPER TEACH?
(1 Corinthians 11:23-26)

The Holy Communion is a sacred ceremony where saints gather together to take bread and drink wine. He performed sacred ordinances with his disciples the night before Christ was taken away.

It is only natural that the saints who follow the Lord today are doing this ceremony because the Lord has taught and personally performed them. The Lord's Supper is, first, a ceremony to celebrate the death of Jesus. What does Jesus' death mean?

It means that the flesh of the Lord is on the cross, and the blood of the Lord has shed for our sins. The flesh and blood of the Lord are sacred ceremonies and drinks that commemorate the death of the Lord. Second, the Lord's Supper means that a new covenant (promise) is fulfilled. The old covenant is with Adam. This covenant is condemned by the law for sin and leads to death. The first Adam's sin led many to death. But the second Adam (Jesus Christ) brought to God salvation and salvation to many by the grace of God (Romans 5:16-19).

The Lord's Supper means that the old covenant, the covenant which is bound to die for sin, is broken, and the new covenant, the covenant of eternal salvation through Christ, is fulfilled.

Third, Jesus is the one who made the Lord's Supper.

Baptism and the sacrament are with Christ and are with Christ. Our evil old desire is crucified with Christ (Romans 6:6). Our sinful body is no longer subject to sin. It is not the slave of sin. We are living with Christ. We have become a new living in Christ (Romans 6:11). Fourth, the Lord's Supper must continue. It must continue until Jesus returns.

There are three views on the Lord's Supper today.

Consubstantiation:
This means that bread and wine are merely meant as the specialty. In other words, the flesh and blood of Christ exist in the essence of bread and wine(Anglican, Orthodox).

Representation:
The meaning of Protestantism today. Bread and wine are symbols. In other words, committing the sacrament is a commemoration of the death and resurrection of Christ. The Saints believe that through the sacrament they are united by Christ and faith and become one spiritually. The Saints appreciate the Lord's grace through the sacrament.

Transubstantiation:
Catholic teaching. The bread and wine go into the body of the Saints and change their nature, which is actually the flesh and blood of Jesus Christ.

WHO ARE CHURCH LEADERS?

What conditions should leaders have? (1 Timothy 3:1-7; Titus 1:5-9) The church is looking for a better way, but the Lord is always looking for someone who is worthy of the Lord's will. The church must have a leader. First, there must be a minister in the church. The pastor is responsible for the spiritual life of the congregation. The minister comes from the Greek Poemen. Poemen means a shepherd. A shepherd is to perfect the saints, to serve, and to build up the body of Christ. The pastor must also serve as a teacher.

Ephesians 4:11 say, "He or she was an apostle, or a prophet, or a preacher, or a pastor and a teacher." Here, 'or' means 'and.' It means that they are connected to each other. It means that we also have the job of teaching Saints as teachers. Those who prophesy the Word of God, evangelists, shepherds, and those who are called to be teachers. The minister is responsible for nurturing the saints.

Second, there are elders and deacons in the church. The elders must take care of the sheep (1 Chronicles 5:2). There is also the duty of communicating the Word (1 Timothy 5:17). We must supervise the saints to be spiritually pure (Titus 1:9). The deacon means 'to serve' in Greek. In the book of Acts, the deacon's duties are to serve the ministry of salvation, to serve the general affairs of the church, and to serve the church.

The word warrants do not appear very well in the Bible, but it must be understood as a 'service duty.'

IN WHAT SPIRITUAL LEADERSHIP DO CHURCH LEADERS MATURE(1 Tim. 3:1-7; Titus 1:5-9)?

There should be no reproach: good reputation without defects of character, "Be a husband of a wife, be temperate and self-controlled, be compassionate, be good at treating strangers, be good at teaching, not enjoy alcohol, do not contend with words or body, tolerate (care), do not argue, do not love money, you should rule your house well, do not be a new adherent and you must have a lifetime of faith, love good, be righteous, and be holy (1 Tim 3:1-7)."

Flowing water is just down the drain. If water is not continuously supplied from above, the water will dry out. And if the water flowing on the top is polluted, the water below is likely to be polluted. So is the leader of the church. If the leader is spiritually trained, the saints will also grow and mature. Just as the water gathered in a place is always level, the spiritual level of the saints is always the same as the leaders of the church. If the spiritual level of the leaders is low, the Saints will not be willing to remain in the Church. We must raise our own spiritual level.

We must reach a mature faith so that other weak faith believers can gain comfort and gain strength through me. If leaders become more of a weak believer, a serious crisis will come to the church.

[Meditation] Prayer is a mission!

+ What do you think about prayer?
+ What is what God wants us to do? (1 Thes. 5:17; 1 John 3:22)

+ If there are things that hinder our prayers, what is it?
(Psalm 66:18; 1 Peter 3:7; Proverbs 28:9)
+ How should I pray? (Matthew 6:5, 6)
+ What is the answered prayer? (Matthew 7:7)

PART III

CHAPTER 20

PRAYER IS A MISSION!
2 Chronicles 7:14-16

WHAT DO WE THINK ABOUT PRAYER?

We want to know what God's will is in our faith life. We want to know what God's plan is for us and how God will guide us. Prayer is a holy place where my will and God's will meet. I pray, but in that prayer, we can discover what God's will is. If we do not pray, our will is to be the first. But if we pray, we can see where God's will be. So prayer is not self-centered. Those who do not believe in God also pray.

They wish and pray all the best to the tree, to the man, to the stone, to the idol. Human beings are bound to exist. Why? It is because human beings are spiritual beings. But most of the prayers of those who do not serve God pray for their own will. They want their will to be built. However, the prayers of the saints who serve God are not the same as those of prayer. The prayer of the saints is a prayer to know what God's will is. It is praying for the glory of God. It is the prayer that God's will is done in us. Therefore, my petition must be not only for me but also for God.

WHAT IS WHAT GOD WANTS US TO DO?
(1 Thes. 5:17; 1 John 3:22; 1 John 5)

When we meet good things, we become instinctively thankful. And when you meet a difficult thing, you have no choice but to call on the name of the Lord. The Saints know well about the power of prayer in their heads. However, few people actually experienced the power of prayer. Why? They know the power of prayer but they do not pray often. Here are some reasons why we did not receive prayer answers.

A student is trying to solve a math problem. However, this student lacks a foundation. Even if you try to solve a difficult mathematical problem in a state where there is not enough foundation, it will not be solved. At first, I try, but now I give up and I lose interest in mathematics. The same is true with prayer. If you do not know how to pray, you will not have the opportunity to experience the power of prayer, and prayer will become burdensome.

The important thing is that God wants us to pray. God is willing to give to His children if they ask for it honestly (1 Thessalonians 5:17). He gives us a prayer training to give to our children. Let your children know how to receive them. Educational experts say young children buy everything they want, and doing everything they want is the worst way of education. Parents' minds who want to give good things to their children are understandable, but this will only result in ruining the future of their children. Your child needs to know what to ask your parents and make a request.

God wants the saints to be good. To be good is not to get the children to ask for it unconditionally, but to learn to pray through prayer, so that the children are mature and have a right relationship with God. God responds to our prayers (Matthew 7:7-11), chooses the contents of our prayers and answers them. Prayer can't be based on our lust and greed. Such prayer responses may be slow or unfulfilled. God receives the content of our prayers, but the answer is the realm of God's sovereignty. God gave instructions on how to pray in person so that the saints who did not receive answers to prayer would not be disappointed or frustrated.

WHAT ARE THE THINGS THAT BLASPHEME OUR PRAYERS? (Psalm 66:18; 1 Peter 3:7; Proverbs 28:9)

There are things that hinder our prayers. You need to know what it is. First, it is our wrong motive (James 4:3). If you ask, but you do not, the wrong is the desire to use it with lust. Misleading motives produce the wrong result. If you have a result, it will be too late if you try to recover it already.

The Lord does not respond from the beginning so that such results do not appear. Second, we can not trust God completely and can not count on it. Do ask for it by faith. Do not doubt anything.

He who doubts is like a wave of the sea that is pounded by the wind. Do not think that such a man will gain anything to the Lord. Prayer is an expression of trust and will to God. To pray to the Lord is that I believe in Him so much. Therefore, unreliable prayer cannot be a true prayer and cannot receive a response. Third, we can not pray when we have sin in our hearts (Ps. 66:18).

If I have iniquity in my heart, the Lord will not hear." Sin interferes with full fellowship with God. Fourth, we intentionally reject and abandon the Word of God. If a man turns his ear and hears the law, his prayer is also detestable.

The Word of God contains everything we need to pray. God's blessing is in the Word. But rejecting these words is rejecting the grace of God. It interferes with prayer. Fifth, prayer is not blocked unless there is a problem between the families (1 Pet. 3:5-7).

For this is the way the holy women of the past who put their hope in God used to adorn themselves. They submitted themselves to their own husbands, like Sarah, who obeyed Abraham and called him her lord. You are her daughters if you do what is right and do not give way to fear.

Husbands, in the same way be considerate as you live with your wives, and treat them with respect as the weaker partner and as heirs with you of the gracious gift of life, so that nothing will hinder your prayers.

HOW SHOULD I PRAY? (Matthew 6:5, 6)

In relation to prayer response in 2, God Himself gave us a teaching on prayer to pray like this. First, we must pray according to the teachings of Jesus. Jesus teaches to pray privately (Matthew 6:5, 6). It is not a praise prayer to show to others. Prayer in public worship is not wrong, but God does not want to reveal ourselves.

Next, we must pray in the name of Jesus. Jesus said. Anyone who asks for his name will get and receive. The way to answer prayer is to pray in the name of Jesus. Jesus is our High Priest. By the power of the name of Jesus, we can boldly advance to God. Prayer is the way to God. Therefore, it is very important to depend on the name of the

Lord. The best example of prayer is the Lord's Prayer. The Lord's Prayer will be discussed in the next lesson.

WHAT IS THE ANSWERED PRAYER? (Matthew 7:7)

There is a condition of prayer to answer. The Bible only mentions that if we ask, we will receive it. If we think about these verses, we will answer whatever we ask for. When we do not know how to pray, there are times when we give up our prayer by being frustrated easily. This is the greatest enemy of prayer. Jesus has what He asks us for this. It requires a spiritual dimension in which our prayers become more mature and deeper.

Those who have just started their faith life in the first place can easily get answers if they pray. As soon as you ask for it, you will receive it as soon as you ask and it will be given to you (Mt 7:7). Therefore, a man simply begins to ask God. They do not yet know what it means to live in Christ. However, as faith grows, we learn what kind of prayer God requires. The Word of God's truth that faith will grow and those who are still in the stage of growth will give it.

The problem is to know the meaning of specific prayer as the faith grows. John 15:7 says, If you live in me and my words remain in you, ask whatever you want, and it will be done. I tell you that from now on you will receive what you seek if you live in the Lord. Living in the Lord means that faith is growing. Then he does not stop here, but God specifically tells us how to pray and how to do it.

This condition is to find out the right way of prayer for those who have grown up in faith. For example, we can pray rightly by seeking by faith, not doubting, praying without sin, not praying for lust, praying for God's glory, and so on. The important thing is that you can do all these things (if you ask and if you stay in the Lord, the attitude of prayer to be taken) is not something that can be divided into stages, but that you need to check when you need to pray collectively.

[Meditation] The Lord's Prayer

+ Why is my prayer response delayed?
+ What is the content of the Lord's Prayer Jesus taught us? (Matthew 6:9-13) Why did Jesus teach His disciples the Lord's Prayer?
+ Let us consider the following in the Lord's Prayer.
Object, worship, sovereignty, supplication, forgiveness, salvation, glory

CHAPTER 21

The Lord's Prayer
Matthew 6:9-13

WHY IS THE PRAER RESPONSE DELAYED?

We pray earnestly to God. Sometimes, however, our prayer can be a slower response. When our prayer response slows, we become impatient. It is easy for us to make mistakes in front of God and people when we have an urgent mind. Look at King Saul. In 1 Samuel 13: 9, Saul had to wait for Samuel. It was Samuel's job to offer burnt offerings and peace offerings to God.

But no matter how much he waited for Samuel, he did not come. At the moment, Saul's heart was in a hurry.

In v. 12, the Philistines came down to Gilgal to strike him immediately, and he made an excuse that he gave a burnt offering in haste. Because of Saul's hasty heart, he is forsaken by God. Even if we pray, when we are slow to respond, we become impatient. We do not ask God, we use human ways. Even if the prayer response is slow, we should not have a hasty mind. God slowed down the answer to prayer because, firstly, the time is not right. God is able to give answers to prayer later. Second, because we did not ask for clear things to pray to God.

And even though we already have prayer answers, we are ignorant and sometimes unknowingly. The important thing is to tell God exactly what we are asking for. And we must be sure of the answers to prayer from God. God wants us to know for sure that we have received answers to prayer. Third, there is something important. It is entirely in the sovereignty of God, based on the grace of God. He is not the one who will give stones to those who seek bread. He is not the one who gives evil to those who seek well. God is always a merciful God who wants to fill us with good things. Fourth, the answer to prayer is slow because of our sins. It is because the problem of sin has not been completely solved.

David killed Uriah the husband of Bathsheba. He himself committed adultery. In the presence of adultery, David could not win the war. God's grace came when we repented and forgiven our sins thoroughly. Fifth, the prayer response is slow because he wants to have a deeper spiritual fellowship with God.

As we wait for the answer to prayer, we experience the interference of my life in God and we desperately hope of God. It is a precious time to know God more. So the saints who are waiting for answers are beautiful. It is the truth of prayer that God has asked us. Whether the prayer response is fast or not, you should not always suspect that the good hand of the Lord is toward me.

WHAT IS THE CONTENT OF LORD'S PRAYER JESUS TAUGHT US? (Matthew 6:9-13)

Why did Jesus teach His disciples the Lord's Prayer?
Jesus was sorry for the Pharisees' prayer. The Pharisees are all children of the same God. As Israelites, they were the chosen people and leaders of God.

But when they saw the prayers they gave, they were formal, judging and condemning others, and all the boasting prayers. He knew that prayer, like a whitewashed tomb, with no power at all, would be a meaningless cry to God. Jesus wanted to teach His disciples what prayer God wanted. And the right prayer not only to the disciples but also to the Christians on earth today has granted us the Lord's Prayer to teach us what prayer is. Therefore, the Lord's Prayer is the perfect prayer and the attitude of prayer that we must follow.

LET'S THINK ABOUT THE FOLLOWING CONTENTS OF THE LORD'S PRAYER

(Object, worship, sovereignty, supplication, forgiveness, salvation, glory)

First, the object of our prayer is clear. We are not praying to idols. It is to pray to Almighty God. The phrase *"our Father in heaven"* Father speaks a special relationship between us and God. Prayer is what children give to their father. Those who have nothing to do are not able to pray. See the prayer given to the idol. They are idols that have never been seen before. But those who serve idols pray. It is praying for what you do not know. This is not the right prayer. Prayer is to bring forth the right relationship first. We are children. God is the Father. It is a prayer that we, our children, give to our Father. Second, the Lord's Prayer contains worship.

"To sanctify the name of the Father." To be sanctified is to fear God and be worthy to be ministered as holy. We have already studied the character of God. Prayer must begin by worshiping God first.

Third, we must acknowledge the sovereignty of God and absolutely obey God's sovereignty.

"Let the kingdom of the Father come, and let the will of the Father be done on earth as it is in heaven." The master of this world is God. God is the one who governs human life and makes all things independent. That is what your child is asking for. The one who can give us what we have is God with all things. It is obedience that brings the master of our life to God, and leaves all things in our lives to God's sovereignty and asks God. We will live according to the word of God. It is like a confession of faith.

Fourth, we must ask ourselves. The reason we pray is that we deserve it. This is for obtaining.

"Today you have given us daily bread," we live on the earth. We need to save from this earth what we need for the survival of the life. Many believers from the Bible also sought God's grace and blessing to live. God gave us material blessings, blessings of health, and many graces. The idea of eating well without God is pride. We can live without God's help. Such a person is a proud person. In the end, we do not depend on God. We must not condemn those who ask God for food. It is rather strange not to ask.

Fifth, we must seek *forgiveness*. You can not receive prayer answers when you are guilty. He who loves God prayed not only for his sins but also for the restoration of relationships with others.

"Forgive us our sins, just as we have forgiven those who have done wrong to us."

We must confess our sins and make a right relationship with the Lord and a right relationship with the people.

Sixth, we must pray for salvation. We must fight against the evils of the world.

"Let us not fall into temptation, and save us from evil." We must disconnect from the evil things of the entire world. We must fight. The Saints are constantly attacked by Satan. We must not lose our spiritual struggle with Satan. We must pray for victory.

Seventh, we must give all the glory to God and pray.

"Nation, power, and glory is forever the Father." God is Omnipotent Creator. We are to be dependent on the power of God.

Eighth, We believe that it will. This is our profession of faith. It is a confession based on faith. It is a faithful prayer that we are confident that our prayer will be answered.

[Meditation] How Do You Know God's Will?

+ What does the Bible say about God's will?
(1 Thessalonians 4:3; 1 Thessalonians 5:18)
+ We have a principle to follow when making decisions on everything. What is that?
(2 Timothy 3:15-17; 1:5, 6; Pro 11:14; Pro 2:20-22; 1 Corinthians 10:27)
+ What does it mean to know God's will and to trust Him? (John 14:15; 15: 10)

CHAPTER 22

HOW DO WE KNOW GOD'S WILL?
1 Thessalonians 5:18

WHAT DOES THE BIBLE SAY ABOUT GOD'S WILL?
(1 Thessalonians 4:3; 1 Thessalonians 5:18)

A farmer would know what God's will for him was. He did not believe in God at all, but he served the church with great enthusiasm.

Then he wanted to know God's plan for Himself. And pray. To know what God's will is. After praying, he went to the field of corn that he cultivated. Then the clouds gather from the sky and it is written in English as PC. He thinks this is what it means. He thinks this is God's will. English PC is to preach Christ, but God has called me a pastor.

I will now abandon my farming and live the life of a pastor. He told the pastor on that week. After listening to the young man, the pastor says, if the young person prays that the cloud letter pc that he saw after praying is to be a pastor, can not the letter be interpreted like this? It's called "plow corn."

This funny example makes us think a lot. We want to know exactly what God's will is. What would be a good answer if God's will easily be responded to the letter of the cloud after praying with the young farmer? We are very curious about the will of God. The Bible refers to God's will in a variety of ways.

First, in the Bible, God's will is not to be seen by any particular class or people, but rather to universally speaking to all saints. There are myriads of people today. They are confused because they have received false revelations. They teach misleading revelations and deceive the Saints. There are two places in the New Testament where they teach that this is God's will. One is Thessalonians 4:3.

It is the word of God that this is your holiness. Holiness is what is distinguished. It is God's universal will to go to the glory of the world, chosen for the glory of God and separated from the world. The other is Thessalonians 5:18. 'Thank all things, for this is the will of God for you in Christ Jesus.' What does this mean? In any situation, God's will is to thank all things. When I am happy, thanks come out easily. But when it is difficult, Thanksgiving is difficult to come out. People are insensitive to knowing God's will when they are happy. They do not know exactly what God's will is because they are so glad. It is the soft limit of human being. It is time for a person to encounter a problem when trying to ask God's will.

When we are troubled, we are curious about God's will. We are trying to save our mind from troubles in trouble. It is God's will that gives thanks in these times. Thankful people see God's good hand in all circumstances.

The appreciation gives the saints who have suffered difficulties once-in-a-lifetime refreshment and a remembrance of God. That is why the saints who are troubled and the saints who are filled with joy are asking for God's will to thank them. Second, the Saints who know the universal will of God are entrusted with everything. It becomes a saint who depends on God. Why? We know what the universal will of

God is, so we can not afford it. We entrust ourselves fully to God with generosity. A person who knows what the universal will of God is does not fall in this world but entrusts everything to God's doing.

THERE ARE PRINCIPLES TO FOLLOW WHEN WE MAKE DECISIONS ON EVERYTHING. WHAT IS THAT?
(2 Timothy 3:15; 1:5, 6; Pro 11:14; Pro 2: 20-22; 1 Corinthians 10:27)

We must know that God's will include my decisions. As we live, we make many decisions. This decision is of course made by believers. It is the decision of the saints. We have to make a decision about which college to go to, which job to go to, which spouse to meet, how to act before the problem. The Saints must know one thing when they make their decisions.

It is the fact that God is on the decision when I am walking with God, loving God, living for the glory of God, and wanting to make a decision, worrying that I will miss God's will. Our will never obscure the glory of God. If my will is starting from a wrong motive, God knows it. If my will is set in the process of walking with God, God will do it in the way of God. You will make a decision and God will lead you. It is important that the will of God is the body of Christ and the church. A holy temple is built. It is not God's perfect will that causes confusion and a temptation to the church. It is the perfect God's will because it covers the glory of God. God has made a principle for us to make the right decisions.

First, it must be based on the Bible. The Bible lives the life of every life and is the same as the manual of life. When you buy something, the Bible is a guide to how to live for those who live for God, as there is a manual for that object. Therefore, if we do not know the Bible, we can not make the right decision in God's will.

Second, we must pray. Prayer is a profession of faith that asks and obeys God's will. Lewis Sperichafer, a Dallas Seminary scholar, said, "God only directs those who are determined to receive the guidance of God and who are already determined."

He is obedient to God and only guided by God. Therefore, whatever we decide, we ask God to save us if we lack wisdom (James 1: 5). This means that Christians must first be filled with spiritual wisdom, insight, and knowledge of God in order to receive God's guidance. For the glory of the Lord, make spiritual fruit in all things and know what God's specific will is it means to pray.

Third, we need sincere advice from the people around us to make our decision. In Proverbs 11:14 For lack of guidance a nation falls but many advisers make victory sure; when we do not have wisdom, we can use spiritual wisdom as a guide to life that asks people who are full. Sometimes, through such people, God knows what God's will is.

The people of faith will be much better informed of the will of God around many people. But there is something you must know. It is just deception that wrong advice is true advice. We must not be deceived by counsel to divine glory, counsel to provoke divisions. Many people get stuck because of this.

Fourth, we must have the wisdom to ourselves. God wants us to be a man of wisdom. We are delighted to be able to add spiritual depth and power to develop it as a gift and communicate God's will accurately. Fifth, our decision must be free. Some people are going to make a serious decision on something that is insignificant. For example, what should I wear to work today? If you are dressed in red, you are so irritable that every person you meet will observe the glory of God. There are people who give a great deal of meaning to wearing clothes while wearing ordinary clothes that are not even more visible than those clothes. Wearing clothes does not have a significant effect on your life.

It means that the person who wears the clothes is not getting a fatal mistake on the job. The Apostle Paul speaks clearly in this regard. He talks about the sacrificial food. In 1 Corinthians 10:27, the unbelievers did not tell you to prepare a list of what you should eat and what to eat and to make a rule about eating food if you invite them beforehand. The Apostle Paul encourages you to make a comfortable decision. He says, "You want to go."

It is said that it should not be judged by giving too much spiritual meaning to the private. The problem is the church, the individual's faith, and the things that have a profound impact on the community are crucial issues that can mask the glory of God. These issues need to be taken with prudence. This is because I have a great influence on the whole because of me.

WHAT DOES KNOWING GOD'S WILL AND TRUSTING GOD MEAN? (John 14:15; 15:10)

In conclusion, we are asking God to trust God to the end. Jesus said, "If you love me, you will keep my commandments(John 14:15)." If we love God, we will not do what God does not want. I will be willing to obey because I love God so much. It has been implied. We must know that we do not act according to the will of God, but that our will is set in it first.

"You do not have to worry that God can not manifest his will to us. God uses the Word of God, the Bible, prayer, and faith to guide our best judgment by the counsel and wisdom of those who give sincere advice to the glory of God(Philip Yancey)."

[Meditation] The Mission of the Gospel Evidence

+ What is evangelism? What was Jesus' evangelism? (Matthew 4:23,5:1; 10:2-3)
+ Why do we have to evangelize? What is to go into evangelism? (Luke 5:32; 15) What does true evangelism mean? (John 13:34; 35)
+ What is the principle of the fruit of the evangelism Jesus said?

CHAPTER 23

THE MISSION OF THE GOSPEL
John 13:34, 35

WHAT IS EVANGELISM? WHAT WAS JESUS' EVANGELISM?
(Matthew 4:23; 5:1; 10:2-3)

Evangelism is not done by a small group of people. There is no the gift (talent) of evangelism.

Evangelism is not a profession. Evangelism is an endless mission given to all people. It is a holy affair for everyone.

Some people are sensitive to evangelism. They consistently say: "I have no gift of evangelism. I do not know how to preach.

"The person who does evangelism is not only someone with special abilities?"

For the saints, it is indeed important and blessed to lead a man to the right path, that is, to lead a man into the bosom of Christ. It will surely be a great honor to God that the salvation that we have received not only from us but also from others will be communicated and that there will be many saved people. There is nothing more blessed than to guide a man in the right way. Evangelism conveys the righteousness.

There is false truth in the world. With false truth, people walk the wrong path. Evangelism is a testimony to them of righteousness and means to straighten those who walk in the wrong path and lead them to the right path. We must be a wise person first to lead those who are walking the wrong path. Just as a blind man can not guide a blind man, he who dwells in the right truth can preach. "He that is wise shall shine like the brightness of the firmament, and he that makes much return to righteousness shall shine as the stars forever (Daniel 12:3)."

We must imitate Jesus' evangelism. His purpose for coming to this earth came just to tell the way of God. Jesus, who came to testify the kingdom of God and the gospel, was the life of all evangelism. Jesus did not use hard language or use academic terms to evangelize. He came to us in a language of that age, talking to people in easy words. And he proclaimed the gospel by witnessing only the word of God purely.

Jesus liked to speak in parables. It was easy for the parable to approach the poor Israelites and Gentiles at that time. They used the language they spoke, understood their culture, and spoke to them easily. Jesus spoke in an easy language, deeply intervened in people's life problems, counseled and solved. They have not solved the problems that they may face in real life, such as those with demons, those with paralysis, lepers, people with various diseases, etc., and have solved their problems directly. And he testified to them the word.

So people could easily listen to what Jesus said. It is a good way to talk about the faith we have experienced and the grace we have received, rather than making difficult philosophical statements as we do evangelism. How did I come to believe in Jesus? There is no more effective evangelism than witnessing Jesus we have met. As Jesus was preaching, he said, "Receive Jesus as the Messiah, and say to those who are children of God," Go and testify as you have felt as you have seen!

WHY SHOULD WE PREACH?

What is to go into evangelism? (Luke 5:32; 15)
What does true evangelism mean? (John 13:34, 35)

Why should I do evangelism?

It is for those who have been evangelized or those who are evangelists. Of course, those who accept evangelism and believe in Jesus as a Savior are truly blessed. The important thing is that because we have great spiritual benefits to us by preaching by witnessing more than the expansion of the kingdom of God. There is nothing as beneficial as evangelism as our spiritual life becomes richer through evangelism and our faith grows.

As we grew up, we studied moral and ethical subjects at school. We will study basic Ethics as a person in school from my childhood.

However, it is no use if you only listen to the teacher while studying the moral or ethics course and end it with it. It must be applied to our real life. No matter how educated our parents are to be taught, if we do not link them to live, the moral education we receive becomes useless. The same is true of conduction.

By learning ethics and morals and practicing them, we become a person. As we become mature people, our faith grows, and we learn a lot of practical things. The knowledge of God's Word, which is known in theory, is revealed in the actual field. There are two things to go into evangelism.

First, we must talk about God. Second, we have to tell us and others. Talking about God involves everything which related with him.

It can be defined the following things: Creation, fall, despair by sin, salvation through Jesus forgiveness of sins, regeneration, recovery, heaven, and fellowship with God. 'Creation' is the story that God created us and created humans to live in harmony with God. 'Fall' means that a human being created to live a harmonious life with God is opposed to God and is corrupted. The fall leads to disharmony, and death is the reign.

To save man in this desperate situation, we must bear witness to Jesus who came to this earth, died on the cross, overcome death and resurrected the Lord. Jesus is the Savior of the people and He is the one who has completed the work of redemption that forgives our sins. Because of Jesus, we must bear witness that the original relationship with the broken God has been restored as a hopeful Christian as a people who have eternal heaven.

We can not imagine evangelism not talking about God. What we want to convey is a story about God and we must communicate the exact will of God to unbelievers who do not know it. Secondly, my story must be included. I bear witness of Jesus Christ whom I met.

I realized how I was a sinner, and Jesus, who came to me in this despair, must testify to Christ that I have experienced who He is.

All of my changed lives, believing in Jesus as the Savior, must be a testimony. People listen to stories of those who have actually experienced things rather than rigid doctrines and theories. Therefore, a testimony about me must be included.

We can not do the right evangelism if we have doubts about "what is there to tell me?" If I do not preach anything, I have not met Jesus personally yet. You have to be honest about what you have experienced. It is very important that I convey my convictions, such as my changed image, my state of mind and so on.

True evangelism is found in John 13:34, 35. It should be the best news of our own life. The news is a signboard that promotes Jesus Christ. I am the signboard of the walking gospel. The love of Christ must come to the surface of my life. Then, even if we do not purposely evangelize, people will become interested in Jesus Christ whom I believe in. There are many who gather around me to hear God's Word. Evangelism takes place naturally. All my life is one evangelism.

"As the Father is in me, and I in the Father, let them all be one in us, that the world may believe that thou hast sent me (John 17:21)."

WHAT IS THE PRINCIPLE OF THE FRUIT OF THE EVANGELISM JESUS SAID?

Every church has a unique evangelism program. Rather, there are too many cases. Evangelism is not about having a program. Evangelism must be a joy. We must be with joy. You should not be burdened with your heart. The important thing is that evangelism should flow naturally from our way of life. The power of evangelism that comes out of me when I become part of my life so naturally is very powerful. There is a principle of fruit evangelism. First, it is sowing seeds. People think only harvest first. I did not sow, but I think from harvest.

It is rather wrong to think that you have to fill in the place to get ridiculous results. You have to be careful about the process rather than the result. If you sow hard seed, you will harvest at the time of God. I am the seeder of the gospel.

Second, the fruit is not just given. Only well-prepared people. If there is anyone to lead to God's bosom, prepare for him. We must prepare ourselves with prayer and diligence in the Word. You can not reap fruit without any effort.

Third, I have to do my best to have the influence of faith around me. You have to show them to live. Many people still want to be interested in Christ. However, the fact that they have been to the church does not mean they have experienced all regeneration. If they had experienced all the new births and had experienced a changed life, now they will all be Christians.

They do not know about regeneration. The church once saw it, but it did not experience the new birth, the joy of change. If you show them to you who have been born again and experienced the joy of your faithful life, they will certainly listen to you as a Christian, interested in change.

The important thing is your will. If you have sown seeds, are ready, and have the power of faith, you must now actively have a heart and a wish for your fruit. We must believe, pray, and move forward that God will. My will sows and prepares me and makes me change.

Fourth, it is the heart that loves the soul. Jesus was filled with a loving heart. If we have a heart and love for one soul, we will reap the fruits of evangelism. The best evangelism is that I am becoming like Jesus Christ. When I become like Jesus, the fruit of the evangelism Jesus has made is also made to me.

[Meditation] Faith = Spiritual Health

+ Let us know three things that faith brings to us (Rom. 12:1, 2).
+ Let's think about what it is that we should not do for our spiritual health. (Ephesians 5)
+ Let's think about what we have to do for our spiritual health.
+ Let's talk about our faith and spiritual health.

CHAPTER 24

FAITH, SPIRITUAL HEALTH
Romans 12:1, 2

LET US KNOW THREE THINGS THAT FAITH BRINGS TO US (Rom. 12:1, 2).

Someone is riding a tightrope. The man came about midway, and suddenly the wind began to blow. The strings seemed to shake and fall soon. The legs are swollen and the sweat flows on the back. At that moment God tells him. Come down from the line.

He said that coming down from the line will protect from hurt. He asks again. "Is it really God?" "Yes I am God. Do not worry, come down from that line and I will protect you."

He ponders and suddenly shouts like this. "Please help me somebody. Is there anyone else there?"

This story tells us a lot. We believe in God with our lips. And there are very few who practice what they are, even though they know the meaning of faith exactly. Faith is believing in the Word of God and not doubting. There are many people who believe in God and who want to rely on people. The above story is an example. Actually, if a person rides on the line, what happens if that happens? As we live, we live our life in such a breathtaking condition that we are really out of our reach. It is anxiety that people live, and all worries come into it.

If God really appeared and said so, then you should not doubt it. But if you do so to test God, no miracles will happen. This is also true of our lives. The moment of crisis always comes to us. At that moment, all we have to do is trust and rely entirely on God. If that's what we need to do, it's a belief in the world.

There are three spiritual benefits that faith brings to us. First, faith calls for complete devotion. Commitment is my dedication to God as a volunteer. In the Old Testament, the people who worshiped God and sought God did not go empty-handed. We prepared ourselves with all our heart and soul and gave him to my unit of God. This is to believe and assure that the people are God's people by giving them to God.

And God has given us the word of promise to lead these people. Romans 12:1, 2 say that we should give our bodies as holy mountain sacrifices pleasing to God. This is the spiritual worship we must offer. Faith is a total devotion and living vision.

Second, faith makes us obedient. Those who confess with their hearts that they truly believe in God, and those who make their faithful lives sincere, are at all times obedient. Many people come to the church to go and listen to God's Word. However, the problem with the church today is that there are few people who obey. What does not obey does not really believe.

Third, faith makes us endure and persevere in all things. Faith always witnesses to God. God is good and omnipotent. God is love. Faith always tells you this. So, by faith, we live in God. And faith allows us to create a more pure gold-like faith through trials. When a person is living, difficult things happen. It becomes difficult and depraved enough to be threatened by livelihood.

Faith is a connection to a desperate hope. If you have faith, you will not be shaken, and if you have faith, you can rise again.

LET US THINK ABOUT WHAT IT IS THAT WE SHOULD NOT DO FOR OUR SPIRITUAL HEALTH (Ephesians 5).

Pastor Billy Graham left the following remarks: "The salvation we have is free, but living in the way of Christ's disciples requires us to give all that we have for Him."

Obesity in the body is also a cause of panic. In order to maintain proper health, we need a diet. There are many causes of obesity. Cholesterol, fat, smoking, drinking, stress and many other causes.

In order to maintain health, there are many things we have to observe, such as less eating, exercise, sleep, positive thinking, and so on. There are some parts that we must keep in order to maintain spiritual health. And there are things we should not do. Anything that destroys spiritual health should not be tolerated. There is a concern that this and this should not be taken into legalism, but just as it is natural to say to patients with lung cancer to quit smoking, it is necessary to strictly prohibit those who suffer from spiritual illness Teaching is by no means legal. This is a matter of course.

First, in order to maintain our spiritual health, we must restrict fallen entertainment culture. This is a failure to live a responsible life as a Christian. Paul also advised me to break up boldly if the bad habits I am doing are not helpful to those who do not believe. Second, all human relationships should be well organized. 1 Corinthians 15:33 says this. "Do not be deceived," say evil comrades defiling good conduct. Human relationships that have harmful effects must be cleaned up. Christians should make many good friends of faith. Do not be tempted by the unbelievers or enticed into their worlds, but rather they should serve as guides to guide you into the spiritual world.

It should not be a saint who does not have the same co-workers. A co-worker of faith is a precious being. They are more precious than friends in the unbelieving world. Therefore, the Lord always prayed only for the goodness of the disciples.

LET'S THINK ABOUT WHAT WE HAVE TO DO FOR OUR SPIRITUAL HEALTH.

In order to maintain spiritual health as a saint, one must first be a saint who succeeds in worship. The Saints are those who worship God every day. This worship includes everything. It is all worship to do things that can benefit my spiritual life, such as praying, listening to praise, reading the word, reading devout faith books, listening to the word (and using media). Even worshiping and witnessing the gospel is a worship service. Worship must be dissolved in our lives. My life is worship, and worship is my life. We must make that kind of worship that we associate with God be a life.

As the appearance of all these worship shows up in our lives, the better we can maintain our spiritual health.
Second, people work diligently to maintain physical health. You will climb, exercise or invest in growth. As you strive for growth, you will maintain your spiritual health by constantly striving for spiritual

growth. For spiritual growth, we must study the Bible indispensably. It must be an evangelical Bible study. You must discern heresy.

Bible study that does not depart from the Word of God brings spiritual health. And be close to spiritually mature people. Most of the Christian life is not only learning with but through life as well as life. Anyone who can benefit me spiritually should be close.

We must not jealous or envy those who are spiritually superior to oneself. We need to get close to knowing what to target. Third, you should use your spiritual gifts well. If you do not use gifts, the gifts will not be developed anymore and will be buried. If you have good faith gifts, you should make use of it to make it a great glory to God and to benefit others.

LET'S TALK ABOUT FAITH AND SPIRITUAL HEALTH.

Those who follow Jesus are called 'disciples.' The disciple is the 'trained person.' There were many followers of Jesus around Jesus, but among them, there were people who were especially interested and raised by Jesus. They were soon disciples. The disciples are people who have decided to receive training. Sometimes it is time to let go of one.

Jesus' disciples lay down their families and set up their own businesses to become disciples of Jesus. They were only trained for the gospel. Jesus still calls us disciples. The disciples are spiritually healthy. Those who have faith.

The German theologian Bonhoeffer said, "When Jesus calls us to be a disciple, it means to come to us and die for the Lord." Those who are spiritually healthy are those who live the life of the disciples of the Lord. Those who lay down everything for the Lord and live according to the truth of the life.

[Meditation] The Guaranteed Future of the Saints

+ What are certain predictions of the end in the Bible?
(John 14:3; 1 Thessalonians 4:16, 17; Revelation 20:1-10; Mark 13:19)
+ What is the Rapture? How do you talk about the rapture?
(1 Thessalonians 4:16, 17)
+ How do you understand the Millennial Kingdom?
Let's talk as we think.
+ What is the meaning of the Second Coming of Christ?
(Matthew 28:19, 20)

CHAPTER 25

THE GUARANTEED FUTURE OF THE SAINTS
Revelation 19: 9-10

WHAT PARTS OF THE BIBLE PROPHESIED WITH CERTAINTY ABOUT THE END?
(John 14:3,1; Thessalonians 4:16, 17; Revelation 20:1-10; Mark 13:19)

When we read the book again in a few months and it is less tense. The more you read it repeatedly, the more you lose your first emotion. Why? When I think about it, I have already heard the conclusion, and the story is fascinating. Not just me, but you too. Movies and dramas that already know the story have less fear, tension, and anxiety because they know everything.

Knowing the conclusion of a story in advance is much less of a sense of tension, fear, and anxiety. Ah! Because the main character does not die in this passage, I already know the story from beginning to end! I am sure. So is our life. Anyone who knows what the end of our lives will be will lose all fear and anxiety in our lives.

God's Word This Bible tells us all about our future. Therefore, those who profoundly understand the Word of God can enjoy the peace and comfort of the Lord in our lives. He already revealed the end of the world through His Word. So, whatever part of the Bible we find, we can meet the prophecy of the future. The Bible explains the end of the future in many terms. First, the second coming of Christ (John 14:3). The Second Coming is the Lord coming back at some point in the future. Second, it is a millennial kingdom. Revelation 20:1-10 tells us that Christ will rule the world in His justice forever and ever. Third, it is a tribulation. This tribulation is a severe suffering in Mark 13:19. Fourth, it is a story about the Antichrist. At the end of the world in 1 John 2:18-22, the Antichrist appears and causes the deception of the saints, and the work of apostasy against God's will arose.

Fifth, the rapture. The rapture is witnessed in many places in the Bible. This refers to Christians being pulled up to the public to meet Jesus Christ (1 Thess. 4:16, 17). Sixth, it is the judgment of the white throne. In Revelation 20:11-15, all people in the world are judged by unbelief. Seventh, the judgment of Jesus Christ.

This judgment is rewarded according to the works of Christians in 2 Corinthians 5:10. Eighth, heaven and hell. Heaven and Hell are often witnessed by Jesus and apostles in the Bible. Heaven and hell certainly exist. It is a prophecy that those who believe in Jesus and have everlasting life will be brought to heaven, or unbelievers will go to hell (Acts 1:9, Matthew 10:28).

To understand the prophecies of the Bible, there are a number of things you need to know first. Is it a symbolic understanding or a literal understanding? For example, Jesus said: Matthew 25:31-33 says, "When the Son of Man comes with all the angels in his glory, he will sit on the throne of his glory, gathering all nations before him, and discerning each one as the shepherd separates the sheep and the goats." There is a part to be interpreted literally in this word, and there is a part to be symbolically interpreted. The literal part is that Jesus comes in glory and seats on the throne of glory. This word must be accepted as it is. Jesus will do so in the future. And the symbolic parts are sheep and goats. Do you really want to distinguish sheep from goats? Sheep is a symbol. Those who have believed in Jesus Christ and have won their faithful lives with sincerity. But the goats are not. Grains and chaff must also be interpreted symbolically. They are believers with true faith and those who do not have chaff. You should not accept it literally.

It is here that the heretics misinterpret the Bible and claim false prophecy and eschatology. The Bible was written in the language used in that era. The vision of the apostle John must also be seen as translating what he saw in the culture and environment of that age into the language of the time.

WHAT IS THE RAPTURE? HOW DO YOU TALK ABOUT THE RAPTURE? (1 Thessalonians 4:16, 17)

The rapture means in 1 Thessalonians 4:16,17 that the Lord came to this land and called all Christians out of the sky so that the bodies of Christians would be lifted into the air to meet Jesus, the Bridegroom. And it tells us a moment when all the Christians are gone. This is the time when the world is suffering and the period is seven years.

Later, Jesus says that He will return. And Jesus rules the world for just a thousand years. And eventually the end of the history of all the worlds, the saints will live with the Lord and with the glory of God in the kingdom of God if they have everlasting life. There are many points of view about the rapture, but ultimately the end is the same, and eventually, we will return to the victory of the saints.

Rediscover: First, before the Great Tribulation, it is rapture. After the sudden rapture and seven years of trouble, the Second Coming will take place and the Millennial Kingdom will follow. Second, there is rapture in the middle of the Great Tribulation. The first millennium begins after the Great Tribulation, three and a half years after the rapture, and three and a half years of great tribulation.

Third, after the Great Tribulation is over, the Second Coming will take place with the rapture, followed by the Millennial Kingdom.

The important thing is that Great Tribulation, Rapture, Second Coming, Millennial Kingdom is the fact that Jesus foretold.

HOW DO YOU UNDERSTAND THE MILLENNIAL KINGDOM?

John who works hard at church school asks her mother, a deacon. Mom! What is the Millennial Kingdom! At that moment, his mother, who has lived faith for over 20 years, begins to feel nervous.

In the end, millennial kingdom? Is it not the millennial kingdom that keeps the country for millennia? Is there anyone who can confidently answer when suddenly asked this question? He is the one who knows the Bible properly. The materials mainly used by heresy are the millennial kingdom. If they deceive themselves that they will live forever over their centuries and millennia, the Saints who have no basic Bible knowledge will soon become deceived.

You must know confidently about the millennial kingdom and make it clear to the unbelievers and believers.

The Millennial Kingdom: After the Second Coming of Christ, the millennial kingdom continues. During this time, Christ and the Saints rule the world for a thousand years. At this time, Satan is bound for a thousand years. And after the last Satan's resistance, the judgment of the White throne is lifted and eternal life is gained.

Post-Millennium: Through the Old Testament era, the first birth of Christ takes place 2,000 years ago. Then the church begins a millennial kingdom that witnesses and disciples the gospel to all nations. Then the Second Coming of Christ is made, and through the final judgment, into the eternal world.

Non-tenure: Throughout the Old Testament, the First Presidency of Christ comes 2000years ago. And on the right hand of the heavenly throne, the Lord sits, and governs the world, continuing its reign. It is not a thousand years of literal meaning, but the church serves Christ in the world, and the justice of God triumphs in the world. Next, after the last resistance, the Second Coming will take place and the last Judgment will enter the eternal world.

WHAT IS THE MEANING OF THE SECOND COMING OF CHRIST? (Matthew 28:19, 20)

There are many differences between the various revelations and the establishment of the Millennium Kingdom, but the important thing always remains. The point is that Jesus will come back. Jesus' second coming must be. The Saints must live with the assurance of Christ's return.

Judgment, Rapture, Millennial Kingdom is not a fictional story, but a prophecy of the Lord in the Bible. Saints will surely enter the eternal world. Whether in the Old Testament or the New Testament, the focus of all prophecy is Jesus. Those who believe in the prophecies of the Bible and live in conviction are those who know the end of every story. Knowing the story does not make you afraid or nervous. Rather, you will enjoy the story with ease. The Lord gives us the triumph of true victory by telling us the prophecies of the Bible. We do not have to worry. The future of Saints is already guaranteed.

The important thing is that as we live, we always have to live with the eternal kingdom of God in our hearts. We must always hope. You should not think that here is better. In the end, evil will be extinguished, and good will win. Truth must surely win.

[Meditation] Go to the place where you leave me alone

+ What story did you hear about hell when you were a child? What do you think of hell?
+ What is the hell?
(Rev. 14:9-11; 20:10; Matt 13:42, 50; 25:14-30; Luke 12:47-48)
+ Why do I have to accept literally?
Hell cannot be interpreted metaphorically; the heresy interprets Hell primarily as metaphor, especially Jehovah's Witness

CHAPTER 26

WHERE TO GO IF YOU LEAVE
Revelation 14: 9-11

WHAT STORY DID YOU HEAR ABOUT HELL WHEN YOU WERE A CHILD?

He was wondering, what kind of hell is a young man living peacefully in heaven? So he asked to go to hell once and came to visit hell for a while. However, the hell that he heard only in words and the hell he saw in real eyes was a totally different world. Many people in hell were enjoying themselves, enjoying, playing and enjoying all kinds of pleasures.

So the young man makes a request right away. Please send me to hell. After accepting the request of the young man and applying for Hell, he finally went to hell. But what is this? It is completely different from the hell he has seen before. He was suffering from a fire and could not stand it. He strongly protested again. It's totally different from what I saw before. Where on earth have I seen it before? The place that you came to before is a tour course. This is the real hell.

This story is made up but gives us a lot to think about. Today, people enjoy living the unbelieving life of Jesus while enjoying all kinds of pleasures on the earth. They do not go to church; they do not believe in the gospel and live in sin. It is to live without knowing the Lord. It is a shortcut, a broad road to hell. It is rehearsal entering hell. Just as you practice hard on the field before the athletic meet, the people of this world are practicing rehearsals that go to hell on this earth. No matter how good the eye looks, and where it looks beautiful, it is full of all kinds of lies and distorted truths. It was the first time I was in New York. Before I went, I was dreaming with anticipation. The world's top cities, cultures, economies, the heart of the planet, and so forth, were all about the city of New York.

By the way, when I go to see the streets, all the streets are littered with garbage, and the city center cannot go out at night. Several times a day rape took place in the city, where robbery and murder took place. When I went to New York to hear it, I thought it was not suitable for people to live safely. Hell is not a place to go. But if you do not believe in Jesus, then the place where you will go naturally is Hell. Lewis does not have a hard way to go to Hell against Hell, nor is it a place of incline or valley. It is hell where it is easy to go and hell where there is no milestone. If this is the way to hell. If you advertise, who will choose the route?

Those who believe or do not believe in Jesus know very quickly what the hell is. If this is the way to hell. Anyone who teaches kindly, if there is a milestone in life, no one will have it. It is a place where hell is the place where we are guided by the iniquity of the flesh without thinking in our world. In the Bible, a hell is a place. It is clear that it is. Hell is not a fake place, but a place where it actually exists. Jesus stressed the Word 18 times.

WHAT KIND OF HELL DOES THE BIBLE SAY?
(Revelation 14:9-11; 20:10; Matthew 13:42, 50; 25:14-30; Luke 12:47-48)

The word hell is clearly a word that rejects modern people. But the Bible certainly has a very detailed record of Hell. It means that a hell is a place you should never go, just as Jesus emphasized 18 times. People living in the modern world reject the word hell itself. People try to deny hell. They say that there is no hell at all. These claims are not convincing. It is like a child who does not want to be punished intentionally denies his sin. It is obviously not worthy of punishment, but it is just scared of punishment and does not try to acknowledge your sin. Those who do not acknowledge Hell do not endorse their sins and are not willing to accept God's judgment. However, since the Bible is already talking about Hell, and the evidence is written in the Bible, no one will be able to excuse Hell.

Because of those who strongly denied Hell, Jesus more often spoke and showed Hell's reality. Jesus knew well what the hell was, so he died on the cross to prevent people from entering the gates of hell until he sacrificed himself on the cross, and by this, he sacrificed his own body. People are not aware of this, and they are still ignoring the sacrifice of Jesus and choosing to go to hell alone.

People think today is important. I have no interest in what will be done. You can enjoy today. What worries tomorrow! I think. But no matter how denied, it does not prevent God's judgment, as it does not stop the shadow of the coming death in life. God's judgment is inevitable and he still wants to turn the footsteps of those who choose the broad path of hell.

"It is appointed to man to die once, and after that, there shall be judgment(Hebrews 9:27)."

The Bible tells the truth of hell: First, Satan and the Cursed are all expressed as the eternal lake of fire(Matt. 25:41). It is a place to live with Satan. Satan's hell is already determined in the Bible.

The important thing is that Satan is looking for those who will accompany him because he does not want to go to hell alone. Hell is with Satan. Let us look at those who are servants of sin today and are slaves to sin. Let us see those who live in a world of unbelief that does not serve the Lord. They are bound to Satan. They are accompanied by Satan.

It is hell itself. In hell, who accompanies Satan in the world, and who receives eternal punishment even though he is dead, Satan does not leave people but is together. What a terrible word? It is the story of hell even though it is alive and hell when it is dead. Do you want to go where the eternally with the cursed, the ungrateful are with you? We must be Saints who cease to accompany Satan.

Second, Hell is a story that never ends(never ending story). It is the endless suffering place(Revelation 19:20). The pain does not end. It is the place where the pain is repetitive once the end is over.

It is a pain that lasts forever. Think of the strength of your body as the pain that lasts forever in an everlasting fire. Resurrection has two meanings. Not only our soul is resurrected, but our body is also resurrected.

The resurrection of eternal life, and the other as eternal judgment, resurrection into punishment. It is the kingdom of God, where eternal life is to be with the Lord, and hell is the place of punishment.

Third, Jesus said that it is much better to go to heaven if the eyes or arms have sinned, even if they have taken it. For the terrible punishment of hell is so severe(Matt. 15:29-30). Jesus still speaks. "Where the hell is so painful and punishment is harsh, do not go in!"

Jesus enjoys His servants witnessing the gospel. Even one person has to preach the gospel and hear the gospel. So we have to stop as much as we go to hell.

"Do not be afraid of those who kill the body but are unable to kill the soul, but fear the one who can destroy both body and soul in hell(Matthew 10:28)."

WHERE IS IT NECESSARY TO ACCEPT HELL LITERALLY?

The Bible tells a literal hell. Because hell is the place to do it. But the heretics hate the word hell quite.

In particular, Jehovah's Witness do not acknowledge hell itself but interprets it only metaphorically. The painful reality, the difficulty to bear, seems hell. I say only. However, the founder who made Jehovah's Witnesses said that since childhood he was afraid of the word hell.

He was afraid of going to hell, and when he created a heresy group called Jehovah's Witnesses, he removed the word hell. So he tried to alleviate the fear and fear that hell gives to people. This is from errors that did not properly interpret the Bible. So even now, Jehovah's Witnesses are interpreting Hell as a metaphor and deliberately stripping or deleting Bible verses from the Bible that are written as hell, and are writing to their doctrines. Catholic example let me explain. Catholicism speaks of strange doctrines.

It is called 'Purgatory(Potential Hell).' It is a world between heaven and hell. The dead soul stays for a while and then sees what has been done in purgatory, and it is a decision to decide whether it is heaven or hell. The theory of purgatory came out in the middle Ages.

It is not a word in the Bible. In the middle Ages, it was a society that traded and sold corpses with money. When the people died at that time, it was said that the place to stay for a while was purgatory. So the priests deceived the Saints by saying that those who remained on the earth would donate more money, or pray for those who died hard in prayer for good works, that they would enter heaven in purgatory.

It still teaches in Catholicism. This is a completely different story than what the Lord has said. In the Bible, hell does not mean emotional or spiritual suffering. There is no place like purgatory where the dead stay for a while. The Bible literally interprets Hell. It is a judgment that the flesh should receive. It is the place where the people who are forsaken should go.

[Meditation] Going to His Merit

+ If you think about heaven, what is the first thing that comes to mind?
+ How does the Bible say that heaven is the place to be?
(John 14:1-3; Acts 1:9; Acts 7,2; Corinthians 12:1-10)
+ What is the Bible speaking of heaven?

(Revelation 21:2,4,6,11,16; John 4:23,24; 1 John 3:2; Revelation 19: 7-9; 1 Corinthians 6:2,3; Romans 8:16,17; 2 Timothy 2:12)
+ What will be our appearance in heaven?

CHAPTER 27

GOING TO THE LORD'S MERIT
John 14:1-6

IF YOU THINK ABOUT HEAVEN, WHAT IS THE FIRST THING THAT COMES TO MIND?

Heaven is a place where grace is determined by His merits.

The Lord came to earth to wear us in the flesh to make us gain the kingdom of God. He redeemed us from the cross and redeemed us as the people of the kingdom of God. It does not contain our merits. Only by the merit of Jesus, we are determined by the grace of heaven. It is determined by the grace of God.

Heaven is the only place to enter through Jesus. And heaven is the only place God has prepared. It is a holy, joyful and beautiful place open to the Saints, thanks to the merit of Jesus. Others (atheists who can live only in other religions or morally good) cannot enter.

We prefer the word heaven rather than the word hell. Heaven is the kingdom of heaven. The ruler of the kingdom of heaven is God. And the saints will worship God for eternity. Jesus said again. Those who accept Jesus as our Savior have already said that the kingdom of heaven has come into their hearts.

It is a little bit of experience here in the world to believe in Jesus, to worship God in the joy and emotion of salvation. Those who believe in Jesus are so blessed, because it is a world that is alive with Him and an eternal kingdom of God. It is a totally different world than

Hell, who is alive and a slave to Satan, and who will die forever with Satan and thrown into the lake of fire.

HOW DOES THE BIBLE SAY THAT HEAVEN IS THE PLACE TO LIVE? (John 14:1-3; Acts 1:9; Acts 7,2; Corinthians 12:1-10)

The Bible expresses heaven as a state of mind. As Jesus said, "The kingdom of heaven has come to you," as Jesus said, "Lord in heaven, our Master." Those who receive Him now have the pleasure of living with Him as Lord, who escapes from Satan's snare and accompanies Him I will.

This can not be compared with the joy that we will enjoy in the kingdom of God in the future. Just as people go to hell, the people who are determined to enter the kingdom of heaven, like rehearsing on earth, enjoy the joy of heaven while living, and enjoy the peace of God in the soul. Heaven is not only a place in our hearts but a place of reality. After Jesus' resurrection, He looked for His disciples in the physical body. Not only was the spirit resurrected, but the body was actually resurrected and met with the disciples.

The Apostle Paul also says that the Saints who come to heaven can be resurrected in the hope that we are, just like the resurrected Lord's body. There are many who have seen the real heaven in the Bible.

These are the witnesses who experienced heaven. God created the heavens in Genesis 1:1 and Jesus was raised to go there (John 14: 1-3). And the first martyr, Stephen, was stoned and saw the Lord in heaven. The apostle Paul also went to the third heaven, which are three stories. As well as the book of Revelation, It will testify in detail about the appearance of the kingdom of heaven. Therefore, heaven can be said to be a place where no one can deny it.

WHAT IS THE KINGDOME OF HEAVEN?
(Revelation 21:2,4,6,11,16; John 4:23,24; 1 John 3:2; Revelation 19:7-9; 1 Corinthians 6:2,3; Romans 8: 16,17; 2 Timothy 2:12)

The Bible says that heaven is a beautiful place. It means that the appearance of the New Jerusalem is as beautiful as a bride who is dressed for the bridegroom. The appearance of Heaven is beyond our imagination beyond our understanding. Revelation 21:16 expresses heaven as a gigantic big city. Its length, width and height are 2500 kilometers.

The spacecraft is about 310 kilometers away from Earth, orbiting the Earth from outer space. But heaven is seven times higher and wider than this. In verses 18-21, the heaven is a square city with twelve layers, each of which is made of golden streets and has a ceiling of up to 150 kilometers. The walls of each city are made of precious stones, and the gates are made of incredibly large pearls. The beauty of nature seen here is just one tip of an iceberg. No matter how beautiful the Alps are, even if Mount Everest is magnificent, nothing compared to heaven.

In 19:9, the Saints join the marriage feast of the Lamb to enjoy the feast, to meet the disciples, to meet the Lord, to eat the fruit of life near the life-ladder (22:1, 2), to live happily with the Lord with eternal joy It's possible. Not only. In the Bible, there are no tears in 21:4. Even those who have a sick and sad life in this world will live there with the Lord for eternal joy and joy without tears. And in heaven, there is no death, no mourning, no crying, and no disease. It is a place filled with the glory of God. Heaven is where the glory of the glory shines like a jewel.

"The Holy Spirit brought me up to the high and mighty mountains, and I saw Jerusalem, the holy city that came down from heaven, from God, and the glory of God was in the city, and the light of the city was like precious jewels, Jasper and crystal clear (21:10, 11)."

WHAT IS OUR APPERANCE IN HEAVEN?

There is something to be done by the saved Saints. First, they will have fellowship with each other. The fellowship in the church is one rehearsal. It is so graciously incomparable to the fellowship enjoyed by the Saints in the church. The fellowship of the world is unstable. We do not know when it will be broken. Even if there is a misunderstanding in the interest relation for a while, we turn back and betray. But not in heaven. The heavenly fellowship is perfect.

In Ephesians 4:3, Paul tells us to keep our efforts to make one of the Holy Spirit a peace. In heaven, the members of Christ and one body come together and have a fellowship that Intimate fellowship and Spiritual fellowship. A close friend is not burdened to have a conversation. We tell all our inner hearts. It is because it believes and understands. It is so in heaven. Saints are all good friends. We understand and love one another, and become members of Christ's perfect body and enjoy spiritual fellowship. Second, we must worship

God. This is the first thing we will do in heaven. The number of people in heaven is incalculable. Heaven is wide enough to accommodate them all. Enough space is available.

All the saints will sing praises and praise God and will add to the impression of worship. Worship offered in spirit and truth is realized in heaven. The worship we offer here is just a model of worship in heaven. The saints who value worship in this land also appreciate the service offered in heaven. We must also keep the thrill of worship on earth until we reach heaven.

Third, we will be communicating with God. We not only worship but also fellowship with God. I John 3:2 say, "Beloved, we are now sons of God. What has not yet been revealed in the future, but knowing that we will be like him when he is revealed, because he sees what he is." Now that we are children of God, but when we reach the future heaven, we meet spiritual fathers, fellowship with Him, and serve Him. In front of Him we are perfected and have eternal satisfaction.

Fourth, we are blessed with Jesus. In heaven, we are graced with Christ. We are superior to angels. "Do not you know that we will judge an angel(1 Corinthians 6:3)," "We will also reign with him(2 Timothy 2:12)." We will receive praise from the Lord. A good and faithful servant, who has done well, says that you are loyal to little things and will give you an authority to rule over openness.

No matter how great authority he has on earth, he is only the leader of the heavens, according to the power to rule in heaven. The power of heaven is great. Fifth, you will receive amazing ability.

Our body entering heaven is the resurrection body. It is a spiritual body. A healthy body, a complete and holy body. We will go through construction like Jesus; all sins disappear, and walk in golden ways with glory. Heaven is a place we must go. The world is comfortable to live. How good is this world? Do you need to go to heaven?

There are those who live with worldly thoughts. But we must keep in mind. We must know that the momentary happiness that we enjoy in the world cannot be compared with the happiness in heaven. Who are the Saints? Those who desire the holy things. We must know clearly what value is precious. "If you do not desire the eternal, you can not overcome the difficulties of this land, and you can not live as a mature saint."

[Meditation] Attitude of the Deliverer

+ How do you feel about your life to God?
+ In the Old Testament, how did the fathers of faith live? Let us think about tithing and other offerings.
+ In the New Testament, how do you teach Jesus to give?
+ Why should we live the life we give to God?

CHAPTER 28

THE ATTITUDE OF THE OFFERING
Luke 7:44-47

WHAT DO YOU THINK ABOUT YOUR LIFE TO GOD?

Livingston (1813-1873), a famous African missionary, had a very poor life. It was time to make a donation in worship time. The grace he received from God was so great that he had nothing to give to God. Suddenly Livingston put his two legs in the offering basket. And he prays in tears. "God has given me so much grace, but I have nothing to offer.

But I will give these two to the Lord, so please use these two legs for your mission." God received these Livingston prayers and added grace to him, making him the missionaries who left the greatest work in human history. "

It is such a noble life to God. As we are presented, we become children of God. It is natural for a child to act on his parents. We must do our utmost to God, not only our fleshly parents, but also our spiritual Father. We have received much from God. We received not only everything needed to live on this earth, but also the spiritual life to live in the kingdom of eternal God. God has given us everything. Therefore, a life given to God is natural because it is received by God.

The life we give to God tells us that we have been separated from the world. Saints are distinguished people. Unbelievers are not given to God. There is no offering, no devotion or service to God. So they are indistinguishable. However, Saints are different. Saints are distinguished. Why are you different? It is because we give it to God. We give things to God, give time, give heart, we give devotion and service. The advantage differs from the people of the world.

IN THE OLD TESTAMENT, HOW DID THE FATHERS OF FAITH LIVE?

Let us think about tithing and other offerings.

The characters of the Bible were thoroughly devoted to God. Tithing is the act of confessing that the center of my life is God. There are people who think of tithing as simply associating it with the matter. If you think only of matter, you can not give a full tithe. Tithing means the relationship between God and me. It is an expression of gratitude to God for all things God has given me, given me home, and has given me the place of all my life so that I may give grace to God in all things.

We thank God for His grace by offering to tithe, and confess Him as Lord. God sees our heart. He sees whether or not my mind toward matter is more important than the mind toward God. God is rich. He is the one who can give us everything we need. God does not just give. He gives the center to those who are in God, to those who live with God as their master. Those who only think of tithing as a substance tend to be tempted by tithing.

But if we think of tithing as the expression of my heart toward God, we can live a tithing with joy. The people of faith who were righteous in faith in God did not offer flawed gifts (Leviticus 1:3). The people of faith have practiced a life full of sincerity.

HOW DOES JESUS TEACH IN THE NEW TESTAMENT?

If we have given our hearts to God, we must give it everything we have. There is a substance to offer, but if the mind is not ahead, it is not a whole offering. Because there is a heart to spare the offering like Ananias and Sapphira. Why do you care about the material that is given to God? It is because the heart does not hold God as the master of life. It is because we depend more on something other than God.

He who does not give the material to God in a perfect heart and in a loving heart is a man who has not given his heart. Jesus said clearly. "Where your treasures are, your hearts will also be (Luke 12:34)." Jesus hated the tithes of those who were hypocritical and eaten. The Pharisees were thorough in their tithe life. However, they have had a formal offering.

Through tithing, faith must grow and change, failing to progress in faith, but rather being tied up in tithing. Jesus is wary of this. Jesus praised a woman. He has seen the faith that breaks the jar with the sincerity of Mary. Jesus' life is a faith that gives me all of his life. If you value the Lord, you will not be sorry for what I have but I can give you joy.

WHY SHOULD WE LIVE A LIFE GIVEN TO GOD?

First, because the Bible commands it. The Bible commands us to maintain our spiritual life. 2 Corinthians 9:7 "7 each one must do as he has made up his mind, not reluctantly or under compulsion, for God loves a cheerful giver."

There is no question that the amount of material we offer is high or low. If you receive a thousand dollar, you can do a good job of giving an offering. However, a person who makes 10 million dollars is reluctant to give a million dollar. If a person who earns 10 million dollars gives a million dollar with full joy, that person's faith is truly precious. It is important that a person who pays a thousand dollar a favor of an offering, but he is not disturbed by the abundance of matter,

Second, the reason we should give is that we are not the people of this world but the people of the kingdom of God. If a person goes to immigration, they must follow the laws of that country. If you raise your income in that country, you will have to pay taxes to that country according to law. Why? I am a citizen of that country. The same is true of the reasons we should give to God. Because our affiliation is the kingdom of God, it is a sign that I am a member of God.

Matthew 6:19-21 "Do not lay up for yourselves treasures on earth, where moth and rust consume and where thieves break in and steal, but lay up for yourselves treasures in heaven, where neither moth nor rust consumes and where thieves do not break in and steal. For where your treasure is, there will your heart be also."

Third, living is a worship service. What is the true meaning of worship? It means giving me to God. Every sacrifice from the Bible must have an offering.

In the early church and now all worship, a living heart is one of the precious ceremonies of worship. It's in the Bible, Philippians 4:18, "I have received full payment, and more; I am filled, having received from Epaphrodi'tus the gifts you sent, a fragrant offering, a sacrifice acceptable and pleasing to God."

Fourth, we must offer because it proves that we are a reliable and trustworthy servant of God. We are the stewards of God. Stewardship is not the master. It is a manager who takes charge of an owner and manages. It is the entire owner's. We came out of this world as stewards. All the material I make is the inheritance of God that God, my master, has entrusted to me. If you take good care of this property and you manage well, God will give you more substance.

We must manage our precious things entrusted to us by our Master, in a perfect and just manner. We must fulfill our stewardship mission based on the Biblical principles of the Bible. The wisdom and the way of all management are contained in the Bible.

The reason I am a trustworthy servant is to fulfill my mission as a steward for the will of God.

Luke 16:10-13 "He who is faithful in a very little is faithful also in much, and he who is dishonest in a very little is dishonest also in much. If then you have not been faithful in the unrighteous mammon, who will entrust to you the true riches? And if you have not been faithful in that which is another's, who will give you that which is your own? No servant can serve two masters; for either he will hate the one and love the other, or he will be devoted to the one and despise the other. You cannot serve God and mammon."

Fifth, the blessings of God can be received by the dream. 2 Corinthians 9:13,14 Because of the service by which you have proved yourselves, others will praise God for the obedience that accompanies your confession of the gospel of Christ, and for your generosity in sharing with them and with everyone else. And in their prayers for you, their hearts will go out to you, because of the surpassing grace God has given you.

[Meditation] To the end of the earth,

+ Why do we need world missions?
+ What did the Lord say about the mission? (Acts 1:8)
+ How was the mission of the early church disciples done? Peter's and Paul's mission?
+ What is the present status of world mission? And what is our mission?

CHAPTER 29

TO THE END OF THE EARTH,
Acts 1:6-8

WHY DO WE NEED WORLD MISSIONS?

The first Christian missionary was a missionary named William Carey. He dreamed of the vision of the gospel in India. Before that, Protestant leaders were not accustomed to the word world mission. No one dared to go out of his own country and show courage to witness the gospel. When Carey decided to go on a mission, many people blamed Carey.

But Carey realized that only world mission was God's pleasure, and earned the honor of being the first Protestant missionary throughout his life and dedicated himself to the Lord's work.

Now the word world mission has become a familiar word for everyone. But there is no need for world missions. The words that we barely knew were the preaching of the gospel, evangelism, and most of these words. World mission is mentioned in the Bible, but there are many words to go to the world to witness the Gospel. If so, this world mission is a Biblical word. World mission means teaching the world and witnessing the gospel.

It is the mission of the world that does not stay only in one place but must go ahead with the vision of the gospel and witness the word of the Lord. Domestic missions mean the expansion of the gospel in the country, but world missions extend the gospel beyond the country. Domestic mission is only for the people of your own country. The same people have the same history. They have the same cultural, economic, political and social conditions. So domestic missions have little impact on culture. For example, we can not find African culture in our country. For example, a beautiful woman should have a long neck in some region of Africa. So as soon as they are born, the hooks hang on the girls' necks. As the ring grows, it grows more and more. Some elderly grandmother's neck is about 20 centimeters tall.

And a tribe is that the condition of the beauty is that the lips are wide. So they are going to live in that state for a lifetime by piercing the bottom lips. This is the difference that comes from culture. There is a culture that is not in our country in that country. When you do missions, you have to experience these cultural differences, social and economic differences.

However, domestic missions do not have this cultural difference. Therefore, even if you bear witness to the Gospel, you can easily approach the same people. World mission is not a national mission but a mission to a nation. So if you are called for a world mission, you must learn and know all aspects of the country in general. World mission is the Lord's way. The Lord is the first to make world mission. As a Jew, he witnessed the gospel to the Samaritans.

The Samaritan Wells had a solution to the problem of the woman's life by talking to the woman in the street.

The conversation between Jesus and the woman shows that the Lord has solved the cultural shock of the two people (culture where the Jews and Samaritans are different from one another in terms of culture, worship).

Jesus is a world missionary who understands the culture of the nation better than anyone else. When we pray for world missions, we should not ignore or despise the country because it is unprofitable and not economically viable. The civilization of the country has not developed well, but in the cultural aspect, every country is equal. It is the culture of Africa and the culture of our country, all equal.

There is no superior culture. Jesus did not discriminate. He did his best to witness only the gospel.

WHAT DID THE LORD SAY ABOUT THE MISSION?
(Acts 1:8)

People living in modern times are called the era of the end of the present age. It is the end of the ending. From the mouth of the elementary school student, it is easy to say the end. What do you think? The Bible certainly answers. The day when the world mission is completed is the end.

Jesus is the one who is thirsty for world mission than anyone else. A mission is a holy ministry to advance the presence of the Lord's kingdom. "And this gospel of the kingdom will be preached throughout the whole world, as a testimony to all nations; and then the end will come (Matthew 24:14)."

The end of this world will be the day when the gospel will be preached throughout the world. That day will be the end of the world, and it will be a glorious day when Jesus will come and judge. The

Lord chose the twelve disciples and trained them to entrust them to witness the gospel in the Jewish region(domestic mission), and to go to Samaria and the ends of the earth to witness the Gospel (world mission). The Lord has commanded world missions. Therefore, the Saints can not reject this Lord's command.

We are all called to do this. Anyone who is a saint should be interested in world missions. We must be saints to join in this great mission that God most desires. I must believe in the Lord. My neighbor must believe in Him, my family must believe in Him (Jerusalem), my country must believe in Him (Judea), and all nations must believe in Him (Samaria, the end of the earth).

HOW WAS THE MISSION OF THE EARLY CHURCH DISCIPLES DONE?

First, they received the filling of the Holy Spirit first. Before receiving the Holy Spirit, the disciples gathered to pray and to be engaged in fellowship. Jesus said to wait until he also received the fullness of the Holy Spirit "do not leave Jerusalem, but wait for what the Father has promised me(Acts1:4)."

Emphasis in prayerful obedience to the Lord's command. "Women, and Jesus, the mother of Mary, and the brothers of Jesus, with all their heart, with effort in prayer(1:14)." Then they were filled with the Holy Spirit in the Pentecostal attic "they all began to speak in other tongues, as they were all filled with the Holy Spirit and the Holy Spirit spoke." What does it mean to receive the filling of the Holy Spirit first? That means the mission is what the Holy Spirit is doing. The Holy Spirit calls those who are committed to witnessing the gospel of the Lord in this age. He does not just call them but adds to them the power of the Holy Spirit to minister to the ministry. Therefore, without the filling of the Holy Spirit, there can be no mission.

The early church disciples all saw the miracles and signs the Lord had done during the period. By the power of the Word, he saw a sinner repent and become a people of the kingdom of God.

The disciples were only weak and human beings, but when they ministered by the power of the Holy Spirit, the Lord was with them and the work of a great gospel appeared.

Second, they did missionary work in the unity. The role of helping each other was clear. If a church is weak, they financially support, pray, and work together. There must be someone who supports you from the back and carries a clear sense of mission from the front. When the relationship between these two is well done, you can do missions that are pleasing to the Lord.

"They sold a property and other things they owned. They gave to anyone who needed something. Every day they met together in the temple courtyard. They ate meals together in their homes. Their hearts were glad and sincere (Acts 2:45, 46)."

Third, the mission of the disciples was a ministry that sacrificed themselves. Even his own life was gladly offered for the Gospel. Stephen, Paul, Peter, and all the other disciples also gave all of them for the gospel of the Lord. World mission is a holy mission to all the saints to join. It is impossible without self-sacrifice. Both the going and the sending person must devote themselves to the martyrdom.

In the book of Acts, there are two great flows in the ministry of world ministry and evangelism: one through Peter and the other through Paul. Both ministries are important. These two are devoted to the gospel enthusiastically. Peter was the chief disciple who served the Lord. But Paul was all he had seen with the resurrected Lord in Damascus after Jesus was resurrected and ascended. What does this mean? God wants all humanity to be saved.

Whether Peter's evangelism or Paul's evangelism is God's desire, one life is more saved and a child of God. There can be no party in the church. I am Peter's, and I am Paul's, and this distinction is not good. It is to unite and exert great ability. World mission is made up of unity. Your mission should be dedicated to praying. You want to know what God's pleasure means. What is God's pleasure? It is preached in all over the world. We received the call from the Lord.

[Meditation] How can you believe in suffering?

+ Why is there suffering for those who want to live according to the word of the Lord?
+ Why does God not remove evil (Romans 3:23)? When is the end of evil?
+ How do you understand the sufferings of Christians?
+ Let us think about suffering and spiritual growth.

CHAPTER 30

HOW CAN YOU BELIEVE IN SUFFERING?
1 Peter 4:12-19

WHY IS THERE SUFFERING FOR THOSE WHO WANT TO LIVE ACCORDING TO THE WORD OF THE LORD?

Among the character of God is 'goodness.' The greatest problem humans experience before this good God is suffering.

Why is God good and should a man feel pain? When we face this problem, God is good, and because God does not care about the suffering and suffering that I suffer, or because God who is good does not care about evil, or even God, who can not solve evil It is easy to drive. Because of my suffering so much, my suffering makes me vulnerable to a test that can turn me away from God. Christians often leave this side of God in this test. Even if I do not suffer myself, we can doubt the living and goodness of God in the suffering of man in the face of many disasters, diseases, and deaths in the world.

Why did God create the world good? Why does not God correct the wrongs of this world? Why does God come to me who am suffering and will not give up His suffering and give me grace?

There are many people everywhere living in a meeting about the existence of God while watching the news of the war, the famine, the natural disaster, the distribution of the unjust wealth, and the people living the unhappy life. The suffering also comes to those who strive to live in good as the word of the Lord.

What we should not forget is that this suffering that I suffer is not God's judgment on me and that he is not allowed to destroy it. God did not create suffering. It is not just one-sided pain. The problems of suffering must be viewed as universal issues, further on the personal, global, and historical levels.

Hitler slaughtered 6 million, he was recorded as the worst person in history, and Stalin slaughtered 40 million.

The problem of suffering is a problem that every human being must suffer. We can think about the discipline of God in this regard. The Bible says that even God's discipline is God's righteous intercession in training the Saints to straighten the Saints walking in the wrong path and to be bold before the throne of God's grace (James 1:12-18). We can not endure the pain, the root of evil so that we can oppose God and leave it to us with greater pain.

WHY DOES GOD NOT REMOVE EVIL (Romans 3:23)?

When is the end of evil?

God did not create evil. It is Adam and Eve who brought evil into this land (Eze 28:15). Human disobedience has made evil a friend to live on the earth. The sin of man and the suffering caused by it are only the result of free will. This is the result of my choice. God has no moral responsibility for this.

We sometimes think like this. There is a time when God may wish to intervene and remove the evil of the world. We are sinners. I am born sinner from the beginning. Without the special grace of God (the restoration through Jesus Christ), it is a life to die without knowing God and being buried in evil, to live a lifetime. If God wants to remove the evil of the world, we must first eliminate the humans. Because man is a sinner and evil is like parasitism on the body of a man. Humans are never good. A man who has committed a thousand kinds of sins, or a man who has committed ten kinds of sins, or a man, who is not good at all, is a child of wrath by its nature.

"No one understands, no one seeks for God. All have turned aside, together they have gone wrong; no one does well, not even one(Romans 3:11, 12)."

HOW CAN WE UNDERSTAND THE SUFFERINGS OF CHRISTIANS?

We must abandon the attitude of relating the problems of suffering and suffering of this world to God and transferring all responsibility to God. Instead, we must try to understand the pain according to God's character.

First, we do not understand our suffering because we do not know what the exact meaning of pain is, so it is easy to misunderstand. This is exactly what you need to know about the pain. Someone fixes the machine. The person who fixes the machine must know the machine precisely before handling it. So theoretically, you will learn about the machine in general. If you do not know beforehand what causes the pain and what the result is, you cannot cope wisely when you are suffering. Therefore, it must be a training that can discern the will of God spiritually and intellectually.

Second, it is important to think of everything from the perspective of God. God looks at us in pain and does not turn away. God always cares about us. He is seeing how I deal with suffering. Sometimes God uses pain. He draws me up in this affliction, and sometimes brings me closer to God through suffering, and leads me to heal and ultimate victory.

Third, God wants to be part of our suffering. What is Jesus' purpose in this land? He came to meet the people who are in the midst of the world, in pain, to reconcile them with God. Jesus Christ is the one who came to us in the midst of suffering.

God is desperate to come to us (2 Corinthians 5:19 "that is, in Christ God was reconciling the world to himself, not counting their trespasses against them, and entrusting to us the message of reconciliation."God does not avoid suffering. If we are in pain, God is also with us. He knows our pain and cares for us. What we must not forget is that if we are in pain, God is there with us. Fourth, we must recognize the benefits of suffering. We want to avoid pain. I just want to get away or avoid me at all. But if we only want to avoid suffering, we can not experience healing or recovery.

Healing or restoration is the work of God's grace. God forgives and heals. It cleanses all wounds and makes them aware of the joy of salvation, the grace of God's guidance and care. Rather, in pain, we can know God more deeply. When you are suffering, you must acknowledge that this is not the end when you go through the most difficult period in your life, and expect to heal and restore God beyond that. When I feel alone, I should feel that God is there beside you, not alone. God wants to live by faith toward us. What is this faith at this time? It believes what is invisible. It is faith to believe in the invisible God. Faith is to stand up to the invisible hand of God when you are in trouble and fall.

Fifth, we must have positive thoughts that everything will work out. The people of Israel have long waited for the Messiah. They overcame the difficult times, believing that during their exile and during the colonial days of Rome, a true shepherd, such as David, who would lead Israel on a good day, would surely emerge.

This is the way Christians think. We must hope that all our days will be well in the future. God sent Jesus Christ to the groaning people in sin. This is possible because God is good. I have to wait in hope that this good God will fill me with goodness in my future.

THINK ABOUT SUFFERING AND SPIRITUAL GROWTH.

Our God wants to accomplish good. Goodness is restoring the purpose of creation. I want to keep evil away and restore God's original purpose. There is no conflict, no rivalry, no contention, just as in Isaiah, but in the nature of the good God. When suffering comes, we must obtain deep spiritual understanding in that suffering. We must get close to the character of the good God.

In 2 Corinthians 1:1-11, we say: Those who overcome suffering by faith have the ability to comfort others. Because I have been in that affliction, I can understand the position of those who are suffering and lead them right. And through suffering, we have wisdom about how we can trust God. Next, through suffering, we are led to a thankful faith. I am grateful for the grace of God who has overcome difficulties.

We must expect spiritual benefits and growth through suffering. Auditing is a complete expression of faith. In any case, those who are already grateful for the environment and are convinced of God's guidance can be seen to have achieved spiritual growth and progress. Therefore, through hardship and suffering, we must realize the spiritual truth and look to spiritual benefits as much as possible in suffering. If there is a discipline of God, we must know that encouragement can also be received.

Pain will bring eternal victory. No matter how hard we are in this world, God will give us eternal rewards. Paul said in 2 Corinthians 4:17-18: For this slight momentary affliction is preparing for us an eternal weight of glory beyond all comparison, because we look not to the things that are seen but to the things that are unseen; for the things that are seen are transient, but the things that are unseen are eternal. Looking at eternal glory and overcoming pain is a sure way to victory.

[Meditation] Faith, Word, and Grace!

+ What are the three principles of the Reformation?
+ When did you use the title of Christian in the Bible and explain the background (Acts 11:19-30)?
+ Only by faith, by the word of God, by grace! Let's think about the meaning of the words.

CHAPTER 31

FAITH, WORD AND GRACE
Acts 11: 19-30

WHAT ARE THE THREE PRINCIPLES OF THE REFORMATION?

In 1517, Luther began reforming by categorizing the mistakes of the Catholic Church into 95 categories and putting them on the door of the Wittenberg cathedral.

The Catholic mistake that he pointed out was when the corruption of the church was extreme in the process of procuring enormous construction costs during the construction of Peter's cathedral at the time.

Luther, the first worship is to proclaim the Word of God. Second, it can be justified by faith, not righteous by action. Third, the Catholic mass must be given in the language of its own country and made available for all to understand. Fourth, it is wrong that the bread and wine of the Eucharist are changed by the priest praying and changing with the flesh and blood of Jesus. Fifth, formal Catholic worship is wrong, and sixth, for Mary and other saints and the dead are just human.

He pointed out that praying for them is wrong. This refutation causes Luther to suffer many hardships. What he did was a sincere act to correct the wrong faith. But Luther went through reforms with the determination "Even if the enemies are as large as the roof of the Worms cluster, I will go this way."

There is a principle of faith of Reformers. First, only faith will live(Sola fide). Luther was on his way with a friend when he was young and suddenly met the rain and ducked under the tree. However, the lightning bolt fell and a close friend died instantly on the spot. At this time, Luther becomes a father when he finds a deep meeting of life through his friend's death and finds out what real life is.

He lived with all the misdeeds of Catholicism and righteous acts, but he had no peace of mind. And there was no assurance of salvation. Among these, Luther gains the assurance and joy of salvation through the words of Romans 1:17, "Only the righteous shall live by faith." And we are leading the reform with the principle of faith only. There is only faith in salvation. This faith is a faith in Christ. It is not a belief in one's actions but the belief that all faiths begin in believing in Christ.

To live in faith is to live according to principles as a Christian. Blessings also come from faith, and love begins with faith in Christ. We are saved for what we do for the Lord and we want to rest in our hearts. But it is not. It is faith that restores our spirit and makes us victorious.

Ephesians 2:8 "By grace, you have been saved through faith; it is not of you but of God"

Faith starts from the faith I repent and believe in Jesus Christ. And then it is made with the conviction that the believer who is born again and lived as a Christian in the world will be triumphant again when it is tested.

The second is only to live in the Bible (Sola scriptura). Luther stood before the emperor. He says that if he cancels 95 refutations, he'll save it. But Luther says: "My conscience is obsessed with the word of God, and I can not undo anything because it is not right and not perfect to repent of my conscience. I am standing here. Here I stand!"

The Bible teaches the right words of truth. All the contents of faith are contained in the Bible. If the Saints believe and obey as recorded in the Bible, they will be blessed. When we receive and believe in the Word of God, God protects us with His Word. When we wake up when I wake up, the Word protects us.

Christians must live the Bible. As we testify to what the Bible says, there has been a history of returning to the bosom of millions of souls. I should not analyze and interpret the Word of God, but let the Word of God analyze me. God's Word is transforming me. I am not wrong, but I am wrong. It is the reformed faith to heal me according to the Word. I have to repent so far that I have not lived as I have spoken. The Psalmist says: "I have put your word in my heart that I may not sin against thee(Psalm 119: 11)."

Third, we live only by grace(Sola gratia). Luther realized that the good deeds of people are not being saved. He knew that everyone was a sinner and that the cost of his sins was death. Luther found a monastery to solve the problem of sin, but could not solve it. He found the answer in the Bible, not the monastery.

He sees Romans 3:24, "they are justified by his grace as a gift, through the redemption which is in Christ Jesus."

Christianity is a religion of grace. It is entirely the grace of God that we believe in Jesus and is saved today. It is God's grace to have eternal life and go to heaven.

WHEN DID THEY USE THE TITLE OF CHRISTIAN IN THE BIBLE AND EXPLAIN THE BACKGROUND? (Acts 11: 19-30)

Many Jews lived in Antioch. If Rome ruled the world politically, Hellenistic culture prevailed in culture.

This means that there was no influence of Christianity politically or culturally. It was economically abundant but had a fallen culture. The city of Antioch was extremely depressed.

In Antioch, there was Bacchus or god of liquor. And they were serving Daphne. Daphne provided all kinds of moral corruption. It has become a center for worshiping evil customs and sexual immorality and worshiping pagan idols. Even in this fallen city, the gospel buds spread and begin to bear fruit. In verses 20-21, Gubro and Simon preached to Antioch and the Lord Jesus and cast many miracles. Many believed and returned to the Lord.

Many believed and returned to the Lord. The fact that the gospel was witnessed in Antioch means that the gospel was communicated to a stranger who had no knowledge of Jesus. Barnabas is sent to Antioch church.

Barnabas came to Antioch and watched the grace of God and added more strength to ministry. As a result, a great deal of work will be added to the Lord in verse 24. As the church of Antioch grew, it became impossible to work alone with Barnabas. So some Esau brought Paul and stayed in the church for a year and taught a great multitude, where the title of Christian was called. The Christian is the title given by those unbelievers in Antioch to those who believe in Jesus. It is not the believers who call themselves, but those who do not believe. This has great significance. It means that the Saints lived an influential life in distinction from the world at the time.

In the fallen city of Antioch, the true work of reform took place. Christians with the right faith and faith have begun to reform the culture of the time and to establish the Christian culture in the fallen city. Here is the true meaning of reform. Reform should be recognized by those who do not believe. I believe that faith is not true faith alone but that it is true reform faith that the faith that I believe is recognized and influenced by many people.

ONLY BY FAITH, BY WORD ONLY, BY GRACE! LET'S THINK ABOUT THE MEANING OF THE WORDS.

As a Christian, there is one key principle of an important Christian doctrine that you should know one more thing. That is what Calvin claims. Calvin speaks of five principles. These five principles are also based solely on faith, word, and grace. First, man is totally incompetent and totally corrupted. The man was blind and deaf to the truth about God because of sin.

The fallen human mind is completely irretrievable by itself. It is depressed by the evil nature, not always toward goodness, but more devoted to evil nature and desperate without complete hope. Ultimately, the totally incompetent man, who can not save himself, must have the help of the Holy Spirit in order to be saved. Faith is not a gift of human merit but a gift of God entirely. Second, human beings were unconditionally chosen. From the moment human beings fall, God's choice becomes permissible. It means that God has chosen to save mankind.

God gives individual humanity faith and opportunity to repent. Man is sovereignty chosen only by the guidance of the Holy Spirit and through the power of the Holy Spirit to those who receive Jesus Christ. We do not choose God, but God has chosen us. "Ye have not chosen me, but I have chosen and built you, that ye may go and bear fruit, and that all your fruit be made constant, that you may receive whatever you ask of the Father in my name(John 15:16)."

Third, God allowed special redemption and limited atonement for the fallen man. Special redemption is redemption through Christ. Christ belongs to our sins and does away with our sins. It is a gift of faith and applies to all who are saved by the death of Christ by the Holy Spirit. This means limited restraint. Only through Jesus Christ. And there is salvation in no one else, for there is no other name under heaven given among men by which we must be saved.

Fourth, the salvation of God is an unbearable grace. God calls us and we can not resist the call. This is grace. Only God's salvation is given to the elect. This is a special call that sinners can not refuse. This is a force of grace. All are done through the guidance of the Holy Spirit. The Holy Spirit enforces and the Holy Spirit leads. We can not refuse this.

Let us then with confidence draw near to the throne of grace, that we may receive mercy and find grace to help in time of need.

Fifth, it is the traction of the saints (to the end). He was chosen by God and redeemed through Christ. Now we have become Christians. It means that God keeps and guides those who are once chosen as Christians. Christians are protected by the power of God. God will take responsibility and guide you to the end. Those who by God's power are guarded through faith for a salvation ready to be revealed in the last time.

The sacrament of Israel and its meaning (burnt offering and meat offering)

The offering was part of the life of the Israelites in the Old Testament times. There was always a tabernacle in the center of their lives, and in the tabernacle, thousands of sacrifices were made a day.

Through the sacrament, the Israelites confirmed that they were God's chosen and elected people, and through the sacrifices, they confirmed that they were the same bloodline and nation-community. Today, this sacrifice is a service to God. Through worship, we become one as a Christian and recognize God as a child and glorify God. Through worship, we have the right relationship with God. If you look at Israeli law, it has a lot of meaning. We must always stand before God as a worshiper. In doing so, you can walk the path of true faith.

WHAT IS THE MEANING OF THE SACRIFICE?

Humans sacrifice to God. However, the sacrifice generally has certain elements that must be present. The first is an offering. The Israelites had no way to go before God with an empty hand. They must have brought something to God.

In the Old Testament times the people gave their offerings before God, and in the New Testament, this gift is our Lord Jesus Christ. Jesus himself became an offering and was offered to God as a lamb. Now we must be driven by the merit of Jesus. There must be a second priest.

The priest is the ruler of the sacrifice. The priest serves as a mediator to help people come to God. The high priest of the New Testament is Jesus. He leads the Saints to become mediators and come before God. The Holy Spirit God helps us. God the Holy Spirit guides us to give you the right service. Through Jesus as the mediator, we can go right to God. Third, there must be someone offering gifts. In the Old Testament, the people come to God with an offering.

In the New Testament, the Saints come boldly before God, thanks to the merit of Jesus, who is the Lamb of God. When such a perfect harmony is made, we can provide a complete worship service. Formal worship is not pleasing to God. We must prepare ourselves with sincerity in the name of Jesus Christ, with the help of the saints, the rulers of worship, and the spiritual God.

WHAT IS THE MEANING OF BURNT OFFERING?

The burnt offering is often mentioned in Genesis. In Gen. 8:20, Noah built an altar to the LORD, and he took it from the clean animal and the bird and offered the burnt offering. The burnt offering is first mentioned in Genesis. It is the sacrifice offered as a burnt offering when Abraham's son Isaac is offered as a sacrifice.

In Exodus 24:5, Moses set up pillars in the name of the tribe, and offered burnt offerings and peace offerings. Moses offered burnt offerings and peace offerings even after receiving the law from God. A burnt offering is a sign of a promise to thank God for His grace, to obey God and to be faithful.

HOW DO YOU GIVE THE BURNT OFFER?

The burnt offering is to take one ram and the priest to lay the head on the sheep's head. And after that, he will take the ram, take the blood first, and sprinkle it on the altar. It is the burnt offering that the rams are carved out, the inner and the legs are washed clean, and the carved meat and head are placed on the altar, burning the whole ram with fire. In other words, the burnt offering is a fire offering. And God receives the performance.

The smoke is raised to God with a fragrant smell. If the people can not afford a sheep, they must bring a dove or two young pigeons for their offenses, one for the sin offering and the other for the burnt offering. A burnt offering and a sin offering are offered, but a blameless calf is a sin offering, and a ram is a burnt offering.

Leviticus 9:24 "And fire came forth from before the Lord and consumed the burnt offering and the fat upon the altar; and when all the people saw it, they shouted, and fell on their faces."

The number of burnt offerings must be given every morning at the gate of the tabernacle before God. The place where the burnt offering is offered is a holy place. The fire of the burnt offering is not made by man. We burn fire from God and burnt offerings and oil on the altar. Through this, the people will experience the existence of God.

Today, the meaning of the burnt offering means the Holy Spirit's coming from God, the experience of the Holy Spirit. The Holy Spirit comes from God. The Holy Spirit will come and be filled with fire, and we will be brought before God as a full-time priest.

WHAT ARE THE CHARACTERISTICS OF THE BURNT OFFERING?

The burnt offering is an offering of fragrant smell. The sacrifices offered in the tabernacle have a fragrant smell and an offering that does not. Offerings of fragrant smell are burnt offerings, food sacrifices, and peace offerings. There are sin offerings and guilt offerings that are not offered with a fragrant smell. The sin offering and the guilt offering are not burned in the burnt offering altar, but some are burned outside the camp.

The sacrifice offered as the first fragrant offering means giving worship and praise to God, and the second means sacrificing sin as a substitute for our sins. Jesus was offered before God as a sacrifice offering a fragrant smell to God for us. This means Jesus' complete sacrifice.

The burnt offering must be voluntary. For the burnt offering is an acceptable offering to God.

Leviticus 1:3-4 if the offering is a burnt offering of cattle, we will make a male without blemish before the LORD at the door of the Tent of Meeting. He shall lay his hands on the head of the burnt offering, and it shall be accepted and made atonement for him.

If the gift of the saints volunteers is not a problem, it means that God will enjoy it. Here is the expression to be praised(to be happy), to be pleased. This means giving it with joy, not with duty or compulsion. The burnt offering must be burned entirely on the altar. Everything is burned without being left out. It means complete devotion and obedience to God. It is a willingness to obey my will in the will of God entirely.

Matthew 22:37 Jesus said to him, Love the Lord your God with all your heart, with all your soul, and with your entire mind.
Romans 12:1 Therefore, brethren, I exhort you by all the mercy of God, that ye give your bodies as a living sacrifice pleased with God.
There are animals offered for burnt offerings. The sacrifices in the burnt offering are flawless males, cattle, goats, and pigeons. The offering of a cow is a pledge to devote to God, and the offering of a sheep is pure and will not rebel against the will of God.

The goat symbolizes a sinner disobeying God before the sheep, Means a pure state that is not contaminated by evil. During the burnt offering, especially the victim's head, oil, stomach, legs, etc. have been specified. Here, the head is thought, oil is power and strength, guts symbolizes heart and emotions, and leg symbolizes action. This means that you have to give all your body fully.

WHAT DOES MEAT OFFERING MEAN?

He who pours oil pours over fine flour. Then we must bring the frankincense to the priest. The priest will take it and burn it on the altar. At this time, God receives this fragrant smell. All that remains in the sacrifice belongs to the priest. And men eat with unleavened bread in the court of the tabernacle. Meat-offering must be completely burned. Food for the priest should be completely burned and not eaten. It is the holiest thing among the offering made by fire. They must not add leaven or honey to the offering of the food. And all offerings must be made with salt. This is a sign of God's covenant. Even when we offer fellowship sacrifices, we also offer a sachet of oil. The cleansing is also a sacrifice offered with a fragrant smell.

And the priest shall bring there a powdery hand, and oil, and all the frankincense thereon, and burn his monument upon the altar: It is a fire offering, a fragrant smell to the LORD.

A sacrifice is a sacrifice of fire, a burnt offering, and a distinction from a sin offering. Both burnt offerings and sacrificial offerings are given to God, meaning that God is pleased. If there is a difference, the burnt offering is to offer oneself, and the sacrifice means to give one's own.

The material of the cleansing must be used only as vegetable material. Especially, it is the fine powder, oil, and frankincense which are used for this material. The other sacrifices are animals, but the food is made of plants.

The fine powder is made by crushing fine powder as a material of cleansing. They make the grain by grinding. To be made of flour symbolizes suffering. Jesus suffered on the cross in order to save mankind. It is because of us that Jesus suffered. Jesus suffered because of our sins, our pride, and our wickedness. By thinking of the sufferings of the Lord we mean that in the midst of suffering I will be broken, and completely renewed as the Lord's people. And the fine flour should always be the same size. It should be very small and uniform. This symbolizes Jesus' identity.

Hebrews 13: 8 "Jesus Christ is the same yesterday, today, and forever" Our faith must always be the same and constant as the sacrifice. We must show an unchanging attitude of faith before the Lord.

Oil may be used for cleaning. Leviticus 2:1 "If any man wishes to offer sacrifices to the LORD, he shall make his offering of fine flour, pour oil on it, and put frankincense on it" Oil means to be distinguished. When they set up the priest or king, they poured oil. It is distinguished and established. In the New Testament, oil symbolizes the healing and restoration of the Holy Spirit. The Holy Spirit has indwelled me and anointed me with anointing the Holy Spirit and setting me apart as a Christian. As a person who believes in Jesus, he sets it apart from the world. It is necessary to put frankincense as a material of cleansing. Fruiting is a costly material. Continues to produce a good fragrance.

This means that it should be presented as the best. And it means my whole dedication, and it means to give the best.

All offerings of food must be made with salt. The salt of the covenant. What is the sacrament? It is a covenant between a man and God. The offering of salt allows us to offer a whole offering, considering the covenant with God. We can not put yeast. Yeast changes food but salty is not. The word of the covenant serves as salt and prevents our spiritual corruption.

Matthew 5:13 you are the salt of the earth. But if the salt loses its flavor, what will it make? The useless salt is thrown out and is trampled on the feet of men.

The sacrificial law of Israel and its meaning (peace-offering, sin-offering, and trespass-offering)

THE PEACEMAKER

The Hebrew word for Peace Offering is the word 'Zachbacheramim.' This is a compound word of Zachbach, meaning 'sacrifice,' meaning 'to kill an animal,' and Sheramim, from 'Sharem' which means 'perfection,' 'fairness,' and 'peace.' These two words together mean a perfect, peaceful relationship with man and God, and a sacrifice to gain such peace.

There are different types of wood. First, it is a cattle or goat. There is no flaw, no cancer, and no distinction. The oil that is on the inside of the guts, the oil on the guts, the kidneys and the oil on them, the ones on the waist and the liver are to be given with the kidneys. Second, sheep. It can give either of them without discrimination. It can also offer lambs. Especially in the case of sheep, it gives only the oil of sheep; here it can give the greasy tails from the sirloin bones and vertebrae, the ones in the organs, and the fatty kidney and liver oil.

There is a way to give. It is similar to the burnt offering, but there is a slight difference. First, the offering of the offering comes before the LORD with the beast to be sacrificed. Then he puts his hand on the head of the offering and puts his hands on it. He then takes the sacrifice and gives the blood to the priest, who then sheds the blood on the burnt offering.

Next, the priest must take the skin of the sacrifice, and the oil covered in the guts, all the oil in the guts, the kidney and the oil, and what is in the waist, and the priest shall burn it on the altar. Especially, the breast of the sacrifice should be given as a 'sacrifice.'

And the hind leg of the offering must be given as 'wave offering.' Here some are given as food of the priest. The priest should eat it with his family that day. And the remaining thing must burn completely. There is a characteristic of peace offerings.

First, it is not mandatory sacrifice. Leviticus 7:16 If, however, their offering is the result of a vow or is a freewill offering, the sacrifice shall be eaten on the day they offer it, but anything left over may be eaten on the next day.

This is a sacrifice offered by volunteers or vows. That is why it can be called a thank-you ceremony. As a thanksgiving, the sacrifice of thanksgiving for the blessing of all the blessings and salvation that God has granted, and offering of the sacrifice in the sense of repaying the vow to God, has a spiritual meaning. Second, the fellowship offerings were a kind of festival that offered sacrifices to eat together, symbolizing the reconciliation with God, together with the fellowship between us.

The spiritual meaning of the fellowship means the grace of God who reconciles with sinners and the love of redemption of Jesus Christ, the sacrifice for Himself. Today, this peace offerings can be called "a type of sacrament ceremony," a spiritual fellowship shared by Christians (1 Corinthians 10:16).

WHAT IS THE LAW FOR THE OFFERING?

1) Offering by fire-The smoke used in burnt offerings, sacrifices, peace offerings, sin offerings, and offerings symbolizes full devotion to God, Symbolizes the shedding of blood for.

2) Contribution (heave offering)-This is done when you give sacrificial peace offerings, give the first ripe produce of the earth, or pay to tithe. This symbolizes God giving to the priest some of the sacrifices he receives through the sacrifice. This symbolizes Jesus Christ being given us in the form of life.

3) Wave Offering is used to offer agricultural products as a sacrifice. The meaning is 'shaking back and forth.' It is also used to mean 'lift the sacrifice.' The sacrificial offerings were the sacrifices of the sacrifice of the peace offerings, the first grain (Leviticus 23:15), and the sacrifices of peace offerings. When the priest gave the gift, he put it in his palm from the beginning and shook it. And forthcoming shows that God gives the sacrifice to the priest again.

This symbolizes that some of the sacrifices offered to God are received. This symbolizes Christ's giving of the way of life to all Christians(John 6:38-58; Romans 8:32).

4) Drink Offering (pouring wine or solitary with other sacrifices)-It is a sacrificial method used in the burnt offering, sacrifice, and peace offerings. This symbolizes the devotion of the Israelites in the Old Testament to God, completely broken down like flour. This symbolizes Christ's allegiance to death on the cross for the glory of God (Matthew 27:46-51).

SIN OFFERING

A sin offering means that this leaves the arrow from the target. It is derived from the 'Hatta' which is offering a sin offering. In other words, it is a sacrifice to obtain cleanliness from sin and to obtain atonement. The sin offering varied according to the social position of the sinner.

First, the priest shall offer the bullock without defect, and the congregation shall offer the bull. Each chieftain gives a spotless goat. Next, commoners give lambs or goats. The poor can offer the dove or the pigeon, and the poorer ones can offer a tenth of the fine flour.

The method of the sin offering also brings the beast to be sacrificed to the Lord of the congregation at the door of the Tent of Meeting. Next, take the sacrifice and give the blood to the priest and the priest will finger the blood and sprinkle seven times before the sanctuary. Then they shall put it on the horns of the altar, and then pour them all in front of the Tent of Meeting and under the altar of burnt offering. All the fat and kidneys of the sacrifice should be burned on the altar of burnt offering, and the remains should be burnt on the tree in the place where the ash is removed. And the sin offering for Aaron and his sons was not burnt outside the camp, but the feet and the meat to eat in the courts of the Tent of Meeting (Lev 6: 24-27).

The sin offering symbolizes the redemptive work of Jesus Christ, which is the redeeming of all human sins by Jesus Christ's crucifixion, death, and resurrection. Jesus himself became the victim of the sin offering. Just as the sacrificial offering of the sin offering was burned in the clean place outside the camp, Jesus Christ also gave all the sins of mankind by being sacrificed on the cross in Golgotha, outside the city of Jerusalem. The sin offering is forgiveness of sins. In this sense, it is similar to that of the trespass offering, but there are some differences. The sin offering is a sacrifice for sin that has committed sin against God, a sinner for those who have sinned against the law.

Azazel: Once a year in the Most Holy Place only the chief priest carries a ritual in which atonement is carried out with the blood for his atonement and for the atonement of the people, on the Day of Atonement, carrying a censer and sprinkling blood seven times. There are two gifts offered at this time. Aaron sprays blood of offerings for himself and his family. And sprinkle the blood of the goat for the people. When they offer the atonement offering of the Day of Atonement, it is sacrificed to God as a sacrifice to the goat (the goat for the LORD: Leviticus 16:15-16). The goat for Jehovah is used only for the glory of God. The gift for the glory of God is first.

If the first goat is a goat for the glory of God, then the second goat means to sacrifice for the sins of the people. The remaining living goat is laid by both hands and confesses the sins of the people and then sends the goat to the wilderness without people.

When the goat is invisible, the atonement of all Atonement ends when conscious people wash their bodies, fire the sacrificial goat outside, wash their bodies, wash their clothes, and return to the camp. Jesus Christ is the one who paid for the sins committed by humans. He was the sacrifice of Azazel himself to deceive our sins.

The second Azazel should not die. It is because the goat for God has already been sacrificed. The wages of sin is death. Because there was a sacrifice that had already been sacrificed for the sake of sin, the second Azazel was sent away, Jesus died on the cross, but he rose again on the third day. Jesus died and rose again. He bought it again and is still with him. This completes the entire redemption ministry.

"and Aaron shall lay both his hands upon the head of the live goat, and confess over him all the iniquities of the people of Israel, and all their transgressions, all their sins; and he shall put them upon the head of the goat, and send him away into the wilderness by the hand of a man who is in readiness.

The goat shall bear all their iniquities upon him to a solitary land, and he shall let the goat go in the wilderness(Lev 16: 21-22)."

TRESPASS OFFERING

It is the sacrament of sin and the sacrifice of sin committed by the celestial soul of God, and the meaning of compensation is added to it (Lev. 7: 1-7). This means crime-transgression-loss, meaning sacrifice for the sake of social sin and all moral sins. There are many offerings of trespass offerings, but the typical offerings are 'a flawless yearly offering', and 'if you give a fifth of the crime you have committed, give it to you,' 'two pigeons,' and three-tenths of a fine powder. In the spiritual meaning of offering, it means that Christians must belong to righteousness when they commit a sin that is easy to commit while living their life.

We are fragile and easy to make mistakes. Unless we betray God, deny Jesus Christ, and sin against the work of the Holy Spirit, we are easily offended and easy to make mistakes. This symbolizes repentance and prayer for the commission of the crimes committed by the weakness of the flesh every day for these sins. Original sin is deeply related to salvation. Repentance and salvation for the original sin are accomplished through the Atonement through the merit of

Jesus Christ, but for the everlasting crime of the weak body, we must rely on God's grace and forgiveness for His mercy and forgiveness. Christ forgives the sins of the saints.

THE ENDING WORD

Theology is the study of God in His character. Theology is a comprehensive study of the Biblical theology of the Old Testament and the New Testament, culminating in the gospel of Christ Jesus. Since Christianity has been officially recognized, the realm of theology has been interpreted and studied by many great ministers.

All of these processes have been the way in which the process of academic development has been steadily expanding the pace of scholarly research in the age, nation, and historical context, so that the theological and academic realm can be accepted as a systematic crystallization of reason and rational human beings. The apostle Paul correctly understood and applied the words of the great Christ Jesus, who best compiled and systematized the doctrines of all the gospel that were seen, heard, and experienced by His disciples who were active in the Early Church.

He is one of the most capable theologians. The apostle Paul experiences his mistakes, the persecution of the Church of Christ, and realizing all the wrongs that he tried to be loyal to the Jewish community he believed in, on the occasion of one event. He has witnessed Jesus Christ coming right from the resurrected light in Damascus, and that all the religious beliefs he has ever adhered to were intended to be saved by the effort of humans. Since then, the resurrected Lord had a special plan for the apostle Paul, which he intended to use as an apostle and theologian for the Gentiles. True theology must be preceded by a deep encounter with Christ, like Paul. Meeting with Jesus Christ is a shortcut to the depth of theology and a closer access to all the topics of the church and mission. Here, an in-depth study of the Bible must be added.

The Bible is the book in which the Word of God is written. From the origin of mankind to the end, the world in the Bible is God's world and God's work. And it is a huge message to a human being. It is the Bible that is trying to speak to human beings. The Bible is not written at once. It is not a specific one that has been written down. The Bible is that oral tradition has become a record. What was spoken and used by the mouth of the person from the mouth was controlled by the inspiration of the Holy Spirit, written by the hand of man from the mouth of man, and communicated again, and was written by another person and kept for a long time.

The Bible is still being rewritten by people who have been living in other worlds in different languages and have grown up in the culture. The great Reformers are also starting their theology from the Bible. It has to be built by a theologian in the Word, a theologian who deeply experienced the grace of Christ.

References

Bam, G., "Concerning Confession in the Local Church", in: G. D. Cloete & D. J. Smit (ed.), *A moment of Truth: The Confession of the Dutch Reformed Mission Church, 1982*, William B. Eerdmans Publishing Comp, Michigan 1984

Beeke, Joel., *A Reader's Guide to Reformed Literature: An Annotated Bibliography of Reformed Theology*, Reformation Heritage Books, 1999

Boesak, A., "In the Name of Jesus: A Sermon for 16 June", in: A. Boesak & C. Villa-Vicencio (ed.), *A Call For An End To Unjust Rule*, The Saint Andrew Press, Edinburgh 1986

Fentiman, Travis., *The Covenant of Redemption: a Covenant Distinct from the Covenant of Grace*, 2014

Beets, H., *The Reformed Confession Explained*, Williams B. Eerdmans Publishing Co, Michigan 1929

Briggs, S., "Church Theology", in: W. H. Logan (ed.), *The Kairos Covenant: Standing with South African Christians*, Meyer Stone Book, New York 1988

Gutteridge, R., *Open Thy Mouth for the Dumb: The German Evangelical Church and the Jews 1879-1950*, Basil Blackwell Oxford, Great Britain 1976

Hendrix, S., "Luther", in: David Bagchi & David C. Steinmetz (ed.), Reformation Theology, Cambridge University Press, Cambridge 2004

Helmreich, E. C., *The German Churches under Hitler: Background, Struggle and Epilogue*, Wayne State University Press, Detroit 1980

Preuss, H. D., *Old Testament Theology*, Westminster, Louisville 1995

Smith, A. G., *Manual Greek Lexicon of the New Testament*, T& T. Clark Publishers, Edinbuge, 1999

Bavinck, Herman., *Reformed Dogmatics*, 4 vols.

Hodge, Charles., *Systematic Theology*, 1871

Ederman, Alfred., *The Life and Times of Jesus the Messiah*, vol. 1

Packer, J.I., '50 Books J.I. Packer Thinks You Should Read'

Hutchinson, George., *The Problem of Original Sin in American Presbyterian Theology*. 2014

Young, William., *Historic Calvinism and Neo-Calvinism*, by William Young, from the *Westminster Theological Journal*, vol. 36, 1973-74

Kayser, Phillip., *Worldview Reading List* 2009

ABOUT THE AUTHOR

Yongjea John Han majored in Law and English Literature, majoring in theology in the Netherlands and the United States and Honam Presbyterian Theological Seminary. He also worked as a poet and writer in Korea. He then moved to Canada to continue his work as a writer and missionary. He and his wife and two children, near BC, are dedicated to a mission for the weak and writing activities.

[Books: *Slow City, The Space, Refugees, The Old Memories of Tynehead, The Qs about the Alists, Refugees Ali, Hastings Street, Epistles from the Drifters1, The Living Breath, The Covenants of God, Theology for the weak, The Justice of the World Churches, Are You Breathing with God? Jesus On the side of the Weak*]

www.ingramcontent.com/pod-product-compliance
Lightning Source LLC
Chambersburg PA
CBHW031950080426
42735CB00007B/332